Hiking Shenandoah National Park

Help Us Keep This Guide Up to Date

Every effort has been made by the authors and editors to make this guide as accurate and useful as possible. However, many things can change after a guide is published—trails are rerouted, regulations change, techniques evolve, facilities come under new management, etc.

We would love to hear from you concerning your experiences with this guide and how you feel it could be improved and kept up to date. While we may not be able to respond to all comments and suggestions, we'll take them to heart, and we'll also make certain to share them with the authors. Please send your comments and suggestions to the following address:

The Globe Pequot Press
Reader Response/Editorial Department
P.O. Box 480
Guilford, CT 06437

Or you may e-mail us at:

editorial@GlobePequot.com

Thanks for your input, and happy trails!

A FALCON GUIDE®

Hiking Shenandoah National Park

Third Edition

Bert and Jane Gildart

FALCON GUIDE®

GUILFORD, CONNECTICUT
HELENA, MONTANA
AN IMPRINT OF THE GLOBE PEQUOT PRESS

A FALCON GUIDE ®

Falcon and FalconGuide are registered trademarks of
Morris Book Publishing, LLC.

Maps by XNR Productions, Ltd., © Morris Book Publishing,
LLC.
Spine photo © 2004 Michael DeYoung
All photographs by the authors unless otherwise noted.

ISSN 1556-7958
ISBN 0-7627-3414-0

Manufactured in the United States of America
Third Edition/First Printing

Contents

To Daniel, Amber, Mikayla, Joseph, Kelsey, and Sarah.
And to Omi, who walked the trails with us in spirit.

Acknowledgments

No book is ever written and completed without the help of others, and this guide is no exception. First, we'd like to thank the staff at Shenandoah National Park who reviewed the book and provided much valuable information. We attempted to incorporate all their thoughts, suggestions, and ideas and hope we have interpreted their comments correctly. As well, we'd like to thank Karen Michaud at the Interpretation Division and Greta Miller, director of the Shenandoah National Park Association. Both aided with initial logistics and helped us establish just what direction our work would follow.

Along the trails we met the South District Trail Crew, who offered much good trailside chat and helped explain new Shenandoah backcountry policy. Thanks as well to former ranger and adventurer Buck Hisey, now of the Shenandoah Valley, and his wife, Fran (also an adventurer extraordinaire), for their spontaneous friendship, meals, and long night of information about Shenandoah.

Last, but never least, our sincere thanks to Jennifer Quint, Bill Schneider, and Scott Adams of The Globe Pequot Press for their suggestions and continuous help.

Map Legend

Boundary

National park boundary

Transportation

Interstate highway ⌖66

U.S. highway 211

State highway 230

Secondary state highway 600

Primary/other roads

Unpaved road

Unimproved road = = = = =

Featured trail

Shared Trail

Other trail - - - - - - - -

Tunnel

Hydrology

River/Creek

Intermittent stream

Spring

Falls

Lake

Marsh/swamp

Physiography

Cave ∧

Cliff

Pass)(

Peak/elevation ▲ Dickey Hill 2,444 ft.

Symbols

Amphitheater

Bridge ⌣

Cabin/shelter ♠

Campground ▲

Cemetery †

Gate •—•

Horse trail

Parking P

Picnic area

Point of interest ▪

Ranger station

Town ○

Trailhead

Trail locator 2 58

Turnaround ↺

Viewpoint 👁

Visitor center ?

Introduction

I only went out for a walk, and finally concluded to stay out 'til sundown, for going out, I found, was really going in.

—John Muir

Located in the Blue Ridge Mountains of northern Virginia, Shenandoah National Park is both a hiker's challenge and a delight. Hiking the park is a challenge because of its generally precipitous nature, but a delight for the same reason. Long and narrow, this 197,411-acre park straddles a ridgecrest that courses over 100 miles north and south, embracing rolling hills, quiet hollows, meandering streams, and verdant forests. More than 79,000 acres of the park are designated wilderness.

To some, it seems all the trails in Shenandoah either ascend or descend, but not every park trail is steep or rocky. With more than 500 miles of trails, the park offers a wide variety of terrain and insights into the park's past.

The famous Appalachian National Scenic Trail (AT) is a major route through Shenandoah National Park. From Skyline Drive, the AT leads 1,280 miles to its northern end atop Mount Katahdin in Maine. Each year about 150 people trek the entire AT. Not everyone will want to hike from Maine to Georgia, but many who come to Shenandoah do hike the 101 miles that pass through the park, many of which combine the AT and park trails.

Human History of Shenandoah National Park

"Shenandoah" is an Indian name, probably from the Iroquois language. There are several translations of the term, including "river through the spruces" and "big flat place." The most common translation, however, is "daughter of the stars."

The wilderness of Shenandoah National Park never presented much of an obstacle to European explorers. In his book *The Undying Past of Shenandoah National Park,* Darwin Lambert wrote, "For almost two centuries, more than a dozen gaps or passes of the park-land had roads that followed packhorses, which followed Indian paths, which followed elk and bison, which followed mastodons."

John Lederer was the first European trailblazer to explore what is now Shenandoah National Park and to leave a record. In 1669, sixty-two years after the founding of Jamestown, this German adventurer—assisted by Monacan and Manahoac Indians—climbed either Hightop or Hawksbill (no one is sure which) and gazed down into the valley below. Other explorers followed, and they were impressed by the valley's rich, fertile land. They wrote favorable reports of the area, and their writings—combined with expanding population pressures—prompted settlement.

Between 1725 and 1730, settlers established two small villages in the Shenandoah Valley. The earliest settlers farmed the fertile and level land at the mouths of

the hollows. As these areas became crowded, later settlers used the marginal farm-lands, and immigration eventually stopped altogether. Early settlers grew corn, toma-toes, and beans and raised cattle.

The surrounding forests provided a cash crop of lumber, and sawmills began to emerge. Mountain farmers hitched their mules and dragged oak, chestnut, yellow poplar, and pine to the mills. Realizing that the bark of chestnut, oak, and hemlock and the wood of chestnuts could be used in the process of tanning hides, farmers built roads to transport the bark to market. Today, many of those roads exist as trails. Farmers and settlers also built roads to transport goods from the Shenandoah Valley to outside markets. Many of the roads remain today and are used as fire roads. Two such roads were used by Stonewall Jackson during his Valley Campaign, when he suddenly turned back Union forces at the Battle of Fredericksburg.

The Civilian Conservation Corps, or CCC, helped build Shenandoah's trail sys-tem soon after it became a park. Created by President Franklin D. Roosevelt to improve economic conditions during the Depression, the CCC provided work for jobless men between the ages of 18 and 25. At any one time there were six camps and more than 1,000 workers in Shenandoah, building overlooks, walks, and struc-tures along Skyline Drive (completed in 1939), constructing and improving trails, fighting fires, and building park facilities. Soon after Shenandoah was authorized in 1926, the Potomac Appalachian Trail Club (PATC) built the Appalachian Trail, and later helped with its relocation. The club still helps National Park Service trail crews with maintenance and construction.

Trail workers weren't the only people living in the park in the 1930s. A few years before Shenandoah became a park, 465 mountain families still lived in the area. With special government permission, nineteen families still lived within park boundaries in 1940. The last park resident died in 1979. Though overgrown, graveyards and other vestiges of the mountain people remain. Along Shenandoah's trails you'll find stone walls that once stabilized mountain roads, and you'll see old apple orchards now dominated by striped maple and tulip poplar.

Natural History of Shenandoah National Park

Though several key wildlife species such as elk, wolf, and cougar are absent today, much of Shenandoah Park is being restored to a more pristine setting. Now protected inside the park, Shenandoah's forests have recovered dramatically. Hundreds of plant species—including one hundred species of trees—now flourish inside the park. As the forests reestablished themselves so, too, did Shenandoah's wildlife. Today, more than 200 species of birds and 50 species of mammals exist in the park. Red fox and beaver populations have increased, as have Virginia white-tailed deer, which were almost wiped out in the region. Now managers estimate they number somewhere between

◀ *Fly poison.*

White-tailed buck.

5,000 and 7,000. Black bears have also returned to the park, increasing their population from an estimated 2 in 1937 to more than 300 in the mid-1990s (see "Be Prepared."

Turkey populations have also rebounded from virtual extirpation. Today, biologists estimate there are more than 500 in Shenandoah National Park. We frequently saw turkeys as we hiked the park's trails and traveled Skyline Drive, particularly in the early morning and late evening. Peregrine falcons have also returned to the park. Keep an eye out for them on Stony Man and Hawksbill Mountains (see Hike 21: Stony Man Trail and Hike 26: Hawksbill Summit).

Seasons and Weather

—Th' fog's ah liftin' on the Rag. Hit's ah goin' ter clear.
—See th' fog a rollin' down the Rag. Hit's ah goin' ter rain.
> —Unerring method of predicting weather by turn-of-the-twentieth-century residents living near Old Rag (still incontestable)

Weather in Shenandoah changes frequently. In the summer, fog can roll in suddenly and bring cool temperatures. Hail and high winds accompany drenching rains. Fall and spring are two of the most pleasant times to hike in Shenandoah, but they can also be the most awesome. Lightning storms are frequent and can be nerve-racking, as we discovered one day while hiking in Jeremys Run.

Average summer temperatures in Shenandoah vary from the low 50s to the mid 70s between June and August. Fall (September to November) temperatures can be quite variable, ranging from the low 30s to the high 60s. Winter (December to February) temperatures range from the mid-teens to the high 30s, and in spring (March to May) temperatures rise again from the mid 20s to the mid 60s.

You can expect to see snow in Shenandoah from November through March and often into April. Rain falls during all months and is usually heaviest May through October. Fog (and smog) can be really heavy and constant during the summer months and can last from a few hours to a week at a time.

Vegetation begins to green in April, when nights are often still cold and the days warm. Summer brings warm, and often very hot, days. Autumn brings a wonderful show of fall colors and is the busiest time in the park. Winter is a quiet time, bringing ice, snow, and sometimes frigid temperatures. It also brings more views through leafless trees, abundant animal tracks, and solitude. During winter, very few services or park personnel are available. Skyline Drive is usually open all year but does close—sometimes for weeks at a time—after severe storms.

Be Prepared: Backcountry Safety and Hazards

In Shenandoah National Park you must keep your wits about you. Begin by getting in shape before going on long hikes in Shenandoah. If you are out of shape, hot weather and high humidity can worsen your experience. About half the trails in the park begin with easy descents that can lull you into continuing farther and farther down the trail and make you forget about the long homeward ascent.

If you are caught in a lightning storm, seek shelter away from open ground and exposed ridges. Dropping even a few yards off a ridgetop will reduce your risk. In a forest, stay away from single, tall trees. Look for a cluster of smaller ones. Avoid gullies or small basins with water in the bottom. On open ground, find a low spot free of standing water.

During a lightning storm, assume a low crouch with only your feet touching the ground. Put a sleeping pad or pack—be sure it has no frame or other metal in it—beneath your feet for added insulation against electrical shock. Do not huddle together; members of a group should stay at least 30 feet apart so that if someone is hit, the others can give first aid. In a tent, get in the crouch position. Stay in your sleeping bag and keep your feet on a sleeping pad.

Watch for signs of an imminent lightning strike: hair standing on end, an itchy feeling on your skin—one hiker described it as "bugs crawling all over," an acrid, "hot-metal" smell, and buzzing or crackling noises in the air. Tuck into a crouch immediately if any of these signs are present.

Stay out of shallow caves, crevasses, or overhangs (numerous in Shenandoah—and very inviting). Ground discharges may leap across the openings. Dry, deep caves offer better protection, but it's still best to crouch and not to touch the walls.

If someone in your group is hit by lightning, be prepared to give CPR and first aid for burns and shock. Many victims survive, even from direct hits, especially if help is nearby and rescuers can begin resuscitation. There is no danger of electrocution or shock from touching someone who has been struck by lightning.

Most of the park's accidents occur at waterfalls. Each year many people venture too close to a falls, slip on wet or loose rocks, and injure themselves in a fall. Avoid wet rocks near steep rock ledges, waterfalls, and other cliffs.

Hypothermia, a lower-than-normal core body temperature, can be a common occurrence in Shenandoah, especially when it's wet and cold, for these are times when all the factors contributing to bodily heat loss are present. Frequently during the summer, fog moves in and is followed by rains that drench the mountains. Other times it hails, and hikers who aren't prepared can experience hypothermia. Temperatures need not be below freezing for hypothermia to be a threat. Most cases occur in windy and wet weather with temperatures ranging between 40 and 50 degrees F.

Shivering marks the first stage of hypothermia. In advanced stages shivering stops, but only because the body is too weak to continue shivering. This stage may be accompanied by slurred speech, clumsiness with the hands, and impaired judgment. At the first sign of hypothermia, take precautions by changing into dry clothes. In more acute situations, place the victim in a sleeping bag with people lying on either side. Feed conscious victims something warm and sweet, but do not give them alcohol. Because acute hypothermia can lead to death, get medical help immediately.

It's often quite hot in Shenandoah in the summer months, so be careful of heat exhaustion. Avoid strenuous hiking in the hottest part of the day—usually midafternoon. Wear loose, light-colored clothes and a hat with a wide brim and some ventilation. But most important, carry and drink lots of water before you realize that you're really thirsty. Shade is easily found in Shenandoah. Take time to rest in the shade and keep drinking water.

Poison ivy abounds in Shenandoah. Learn to identify this plant and avoid plants with shiny leaves in groups of three. (According to an old adage, "Leaves of three, let it be.") In the fall, poison ivy turns a beautiful orange and the plant produces a white berry (see Appendix B: Further Reading for a recommended field guide to plants).

We recommend you wear long pants and long sleeves while hiking in Shenandoah. Trails are sometimes narrow, and it's easy to get poison ivy oil on your skin and clothing. Use care when selecting "cat holes" for bodily wastes. Rashes on the genitals can be particularly troublesome and may require medical attention.

If you have or may have touched poison ivy, wash the area immediately with water. Washing within the first ten minutes often can prevent irritation. Ideally, you should place suspect clothing in plastic bags until it can be thoroughly washed to remove irritating oils. If a rash appears, apply calamine or Caladryl lotion. Persistent rashes may require something stronger, such as a salve containing cortisone. Extreme cases may require a cortisone injection.

Most waters in Shenandoah appear refreshing but may contain a microorganism called *Giardia lamblia,* which can cause severe diarrhea and dehydration in humans. Mammals—especially beavers—spread this nasty parasite through their feces. Water can be rendered safe by boiling it for at least five minutes or by passing it through a filter system with a mesh no larger than 5 micrometers. According to some experts, iodine tablets and other purification additives are not considered effective against *Giardia.* Any surface water supply is a potential source of this organism, and hikers who drink directly from streams and springs risk contracting "beaver fever" and its painful symptoms.

Biting insects—mosquitoes, gnats, and flies—can ruin a trip. Be prepared with an effective repellent that you have tried ahead of time. It is too late when you are on the trail to discover that the repellent is more irritating than the bugs. DEET is the active ingredient in most repellents. However, prolonged overuse of a solution of 30 percent DEET can cause some negative reactions, particularly in children.

In Shenandoah the incidence of Lyme disease, caused by a parasitic microorganism carried by ticks, is low. Ticks, however, are numerous, and contact with them makes it possible to contract Lyme disease, Rocky Mountain spotted fever, and the human *Granulocytic ehrlichia* infection. Ticks can appear any time of the year at temperatures above 50 degrees F—even in January and February. When they attach to the skin, ticks secrete a saliva that thins the blood and they begin to feed. At the same time, they may inject a disease-carrying parasite. General symptoms of tick-borne diseases include fever with shaking chills and severe muscle pain. Lyme disease may produce a rash on the palms and soles, which later spreads to the whole body.

The best way to keep from getting the disease is to prevent ticks from attaching to your skin. Wear long pants and tuck them into your boots or bind the bottoms with a loose rubber band. Wear long-sleeve shirts. Consider applying a spray containing DEET to your skin and clothing. Some manufacturers sell a tick spray (for clothing only), and it seems to work well when sprayed on pants legs and boots. At the end of the day, conduct a tick search, and don't panic if you find one. The process of transmitting the disease takes hours.

To remove a loose tick, flick it off with a fingernail. If the tick is firmly embedded, hold a hot, recently extinguished match head to the tick's back. If the tick does not let go, use tweezers to pinch a small area around the tick's mouth and pull it out. Try not to squeeze the tick's body as this increases the risk of infection. Finally, clean the area with an antiseptic.

Rattlesnakes are common in Shenandoah, but during the months we spent gathering information for this book, we encountered only two. You should always remain alert to the presence of snakes. If you've never heard a rattlesnake rattle, don't worry—the sound is unmistakable. Rattlers strike when they're angry, and someone in Shenandoah has been bitten every few years, although no deaths have been reported. Snake venom is relatively slow acting, a fact that allows victims time to get medical help.

Learning to avoid snakes and their bites is relatively simple. Watch where you step and where you sit down, particularly in rocky areas. Avoid hiking at night. Snakes generally hole up by day, then bask on sun-warmed rocks or sand when temperatures cool in the evening; they generally hunt at night, so it is best to sleep in tents with sewn-in floors and zippered doors.

Before hiking in snake country, become familiar with first-aid treatment for bites. Commercial snake-venom extractors are great if used within the first three minutes. Victims—if alone—should walk slowly to the trailhead and seek immediate attention. If you are accompanying a snake-bite victim, anticipate and treat for shock as needed.

Copperheads, the other poisonous snake in Shenandoah, are said to be common, though we never saw one. They usually have yellow spots with black markings that tend to make them fade into their surroundings in mottled light. (See Appendix B: Further Reading for a recommended field guide to snakes.)

Use proper precautions to avoid trouble with black bears in Shenandoah National Park. *Never keep your food in your tent.* In the backcountry, string it from a high branch, ideally in sealed containers. When you obtain your free backcountry permit, the park gives you specific height and distance requirements for hanging food. Never cook in your tent. *If you encounter a black bear while hiking, do not run.* Black bears are generally intimidated by noise and an upright stance. *Clap and shout to let the bear know where you are. If the noise doesn't scare the bruin, quietly back off from a potential encounter.* For more information on coexisting with bears in the backcountry, see The Globe Pequot Press's *Bear Aware* by Bill Schneider.

Shenandoah rangers say falling trees pose a greater risk now than they have for many decades. Gypsy moth infestations and violent storms have resulted in rotten roots and dead trees ready to topple in many locations in the park. Be watchful of dead trees when you're on the trail—especially in high winds—and be careful where you pitch your tent.

Plan hikes within your group's physical ability. Do not attempt hikes or backpacking segments that are more than you and your group can safely accomplish in daylight. Know the terrain. Before departing, study the maps. Hiking after dark is not only uncomfortable but also dangerous, especially if you are not familiar with the topography and trail conditions.

Always leave an itinerary of your hike with someone before you leave. It should include where you will park, a description of your car and license plate numbers, where you will be hiking, when you expect to complete the trip, and who to contact in case of emergency. If you have questions before you leave, ask park rangers.

If you plan to backpack overnight, make sure you first acquire a free backcountry permit, available from the park's two visitor centers, at ranger stations, and at park entrances.

Parts of Shenandoah can be used by both hikers and horseback riders. Such trails are marked with yellow blazes, and horses have the right-of-way on them. Hikers should yield to all stock and riders. If you encounter stock on the trail, move quietly to the lower side of the trail to let the stock pass. To avoid spooking horses, make your presence known.

Backcountry Essentials

Comfortable clothes and footwear will do a lot to make your hike pleasant. In cool weather, dress in layers, first in a light, inner layer made of material, such as polypropylene, that will wick moisture away from your skin. Next, wear a warmer, porous layer that can be removed if necessary. Over that, wear an outer layer that is windproof and rainproof. Layers allow you to regulate your temperature by putting on or taking off layers as the weather and exertion dictate. A good poncho or raincoat is standard backpacking equipment, especially in Shenandoah, where rain, snow, sleet, and hail are frequent and unpredictable.

Hiking boots should be sturdy and supportive and have good soles. Many people wear heavy leather boots, while others prefer lighter-weight boots with breathable, water-resistant fabrics. If you are a beginner, visit your local outdoor sporting goods store and try on different boots. Several good books on hiking equipment, including Colin Fletcher's *The Complete Walker,* are listed in Appendix B: Further Reading.

Backcountry camping is available throughout most of the park with a permit. Stays are limited to two nights at any one site or fourteen consecutive nights in the backcountry. All campers must obtain a free backcountry camping permit from visitor contact stations during business hours or by writing the park superintendent's office (see Appendix A: For More Information). Include your name, complete address, entry and exit dates of trip, number in party, and trip itinerary. Maximum group size for backcountry trips is ten. Some trails are closed to backcountry camping. Park Service officials will give you these and other regulations when you receive your permit. (For suggestions on minimum-impact camping, see "Zero Impact.")

Hiking with children can be enjoyable for the whole family. Kids see the world from a different perspective—it's the little things adults barely notice that are so special to children: bugs scampering across the trail, spiderwebs dripping with morning dew, or lizards doing pushups on a trailside boulder. Kids love to splash rocks into a lake, watch sticks run the rapids of a mountain stream, and explore animal tracks in the sand.

To make the trip fun for children let the young ones set the pace. Until your children are able to keep up on extended hikes, forget about 30-mile treks to a favorite backcountry campsite. Instead, plan a destination only a mile or two from the trailhead. Children tire quickly and become easily sidetracked, so don't be surprised if you don't make it to your destination. Plan alternative campsites en route to your final camp.

Help children enjoy the hike and learn about what they see. Always point out special things along the trail. Help them anticipate what is around the next bend—perhaps a waterfall, or a pond filled with wriggling tadpoles. Make the hike fun and interesting, and kids will keep going.

Young skin is very sensitive to the sun, so always carry a strong sunscreen and use it on sunny days. A good bug repellent, preferably a natural product, should be a standard part of your first-aid kit. Also, carry a product that helps take the itch and sting out of bug bites. A hat helps keep the sun out of sensitive young eyes. Rain gear is also an important consideration. Children generally have less tolerance to cold than adults, so ample clothing is important.

Parents with young children must, of course, carry plenty of diapers—and pack them out when leaving. Some children can get wet at night, so extra sleeping clothes and a waterproof pad are must-haves. To alleviate extra weight, parents with very young children can pack lightweight and inexpensive dry baby foods to which only water needs to be added.

Make your children aware of what poison ivy looks like and warn them not to touch it. Be especially watchful for stinging insects—wasps, hornets, and bees—and examine your children carefully and often for ticks.

Children learn from their parents by example. Hiking and camping trips are excellent opportunities to teach young ones to tread lightly and minimize their impact on the environment.

Zero Impact

Few experiences are more irritating or distasteful than finding aluminum cans, candy wrappers, and other trash along the trail. If you can pack it in, you can pack it out. Some people take an extra garbage bag on hikes just to pick up litter left by inconsiderate trekkers. A clean trail is less inviting to the litterer.

Modern, lightweight camp stoves and lanterns eliminate the need for campfires and the stone fire rings left behind. Open fires, in fact, are prohibited in Shenandoah. Backpacking stoves are ideal for wilderness camping and for brewing a hot cup of coffee or bowl of soup. For more information on minimum-impact hiking and camping methods, ask local rangers or see The Globe Pequot Press's *Leave No Trace* by Will Harmon.

Hiker's Checklist

The following list serves as a suggestion of the types of items you may want to include in your day pack. For instance, the male partner in the current authorial team shows some tendency to swell following bee stings, so he always includes an antihistamine. Most people, in fact, react to bug bites; and since body chemistry changes from year to year, you should always take along some type of antihistamine. Customize the first-aid container in your day pack and backpack to meet your own specific needs.

First-Aid Equipment and Supplies

- ❏ Waterproof plastic bag to hold your entire first-aid kit
- ❏ Bandages
- ❏ Adhesive tape
- ❏ Gauze and/or gauze compresses
- ❏ Elastic bandage
- ❏ Aspirin or other pain medication
- ❏ Antibacterial ointment
- ❏ Benadryl for allergic response
- ❏ Small packet of meat tenderizer to treat insect stings
- ❏ Mild laxative
- ❏ Antidiarrheal medication
- ❏ Compact snakebite kit that includes an efficient suction device
- ❏ Moleskin
- ❏ Needles
- ❏ Scissors, or a Swiss Army knife with scissors

Survival Kit

- ❏ Space blanket or large garbage bag
- ❏ Whistle
- ❏ Waterproof matches and/or a reliable cigarette lighter
- ❏ Compass
- ❏ Maps
- ❏ Extra high-energy food bars
- ❏ 10 to 20 feet of light nylon rope
- ❏ Small flashlight

How to Use This Guide

More than 500 miles of trails wander through Shenandoah National Park, and knowing where to start can be difficult. This guide will help you select trails based on your abilities and interests. With that goal in mind, we spent three months hiking nearly all of the trails in the park. In Shenandoah we often found that the aesthetics of the area's

incredible natural history, as well as its human history, provided compelling reasons to hike these trails.

Even though we hiked nearly every trail, we did not write about them all. We made as many loops as possible because most hikers won't have drop-offs or pick-ups. With a good topo map (listed in each hike description) and this guide in hand, you can easily choose your own loops or one-way hikes.

There are mileposts on the west side of Skyline Drive. Because almost all trails originate from this road, it's very simple to find your desired trailhead. Skyline Mile 0.0 begins at the north entrance to the park, near the town of Front Royal. Rockfish Gap provides the site for the last milepost, located at Mile 105 in the south. From there, U.S. Highway 250 and Interstate 64 go west to the town of Waynesboro, at the bottom of the mountain as you leave the park.

Trails marked by blue blazes are for hikers only; those with yellow blazes indicate horse trails and may also be used by hikers. The famous Appalachian Trail (hikers only) uses white blazes. Most blazes are found on trees, but in many areas they're found on rocks and are easily seen.

Hike descriptions include **Distance and Difficulty.** *Easy* trails can be completed without difficulty by hikers of all abilities. Hikes rated *moderate* will challenge novices. *Moderately strenuous* hikes will tax even experienced hikers, and *strenuous* trails will push the limits of the most Herculean hiker. The **Traffic** section indicates how much use a route receives. Trails receiving *light* use offer an 80-percent probability of meeting one or two parties in a day. *Moderate* traffic indicates an 80-percent chance of meeting three or more parties, while *heavy*-use trails offer an 80-percent probability of seeing five or more other groups. Trails receiving heavy use are usually muddy in wet weather. This is a general assessment; the information here will vary by season, month, and even day of the week. Hike descriptions also give the **Maps** required for the hike and **Finding the trailhead** directions.

The **Miles and Directions** section highlights landmarks, trail junctions, and gradient changes. Distances were derived using a planimeter, which measures two-dimensional distances on a topographical map. These distances were then corrected for altitude gain or loss and were further modified when managers made more precise determinations. Nevertheless, the resulting mileages should be considered conservative estimates because they do not always account for small-scale twists and turns or minor ups and downs.

The **Hike** section includes geologic and ecological features, fishing opportunities, campsites, and other important information. Photographs have been included to give you a visual preview of some of the prominent features seen along the trail.

Where appropriate, an elevation profile accompanies each trail description and provides a general overview of major elevation gains and losses. Elevation profiles

White blazes like these are often seen along the Appalachian Trail.

were not included for trails where elevation gains and losses are insignificant. The profiles depict the ups and downs of the hikes, with miles on the horizontal axis and elevation (feet above sea level) on the vertical axis. Elevation increments vary depending upon the hike's steepness. Some short dips and climbs (especially those less than 500 feet) may not show on the profiles. Elevation lines are adjusted to fit onto the graph and do not necessarily reflect the actual trail-slope angle.

For the most part, use this guide in conjunction with topographical maps or other maps, as indicated. If you refer to all the information provided, you will be prepared for the pleasures and pitfalls of hiking Shenandoah National Park.

Knowledge of a few special terms will help you understand the geography of Shenandoah National Park: A *gap* is a mountain pass, a *hollow* is a valley, and a *run* is a small stream or brook.

About the Maps

The maps in this book use elevation tints called hypsometry, to portray relief. Each gray tone represents a range of equal elevation, as shown in the scale key with the map. These maps will give you a good idea of elevation gain and loss. the darker tones are lower elevations and the lighter grays are higher elevations. The lighter the tone, the higher the elevation. Narrow bands of different gray tones spaced closely together indicate steep terrain, whereas wider bands indicate areas of more gradual slope.

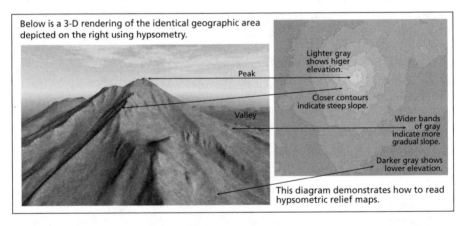

Below is a 3-D rendering of the identical geographic area depicted on the right using hypsometry.

Lighter gray shows higer elevation.

Peak

Closer contours indicate steep slope.

Valley

Wider bands of gray indicate more gradual slope.

Darker gray shows lower elevation.

This diagram demonstrates how to read hypsometric relief maps.

North District
Skyline Mile 0.0 to 31.5

You can easily reach the North District of Shenandoah from Front Royal, Virginia, by leaving U.S. Highway 340 south of town and following the frequent signs to the park's entrance. The park's northern entrance station is less than a mile from US 340. The Dickey Ridge Visitor Center is at Mile 4.6 on Skyline Drive and is worth a stop. The visitor center is the starting point of several trails in this guide.

One of the park's first trails provides a commanding view of Massanutten Mountain and several of the various peaks composing the northern end of its range. From Dickey Hill, you can see Signal Knob, a mountain that served as a lookout during the Civil War. The northern portion of the park offers other reminders of the war, and hiking is a good way to step back to that time.

During the Civil War, Marcus Buck watched the Battle of Overall Run from a lookout post in the northern portion of what is now Shenandoah National Park. "It was a very spectacular affair," wrote Buck in his diary, "to look down on men riding, charging and firing their carbines and pistols."

The Appalachian Trail (AT) enters the park along its eastern border about 6 miles south of the entrance station. It first crosses Skyline Drive at Mile 10.4 near Compton Gap and is an integral part of many hikes in this guide.

1 Dickey Ridge Trail

The most northern trail in the park, this one-way path leads past old homesteads and a stream, climbs Dickey Ridge, and terminates at Mile 10.4 on Skyline Drive (Compton Gap).

Skyline Mile: 0.05
Distance: 10.3 miles, one way; shuttle optional.
Difficulty: Easy to moderately strenuous.
Traffic: Light to moderate.

Maps: National Geographic Trails Illustrated Topographic Map 228; Map 9, Appalachian Trail and Other Trails in Shenandoah National Park, North District (PATC, Inc.).

Finding the trailhead: The Dickey Ridge Trail begins on the south end of Front Royal on U.S. Highway 340. As soon as you get on Skyline Drive, before the park entrance gate, you will see a small parking area on the road to the right (west). The cement post marking the Dickey Ridge Trail stands right beside the parking area.

The Hike

This is one hike where you use your own discretion on the length. If you wish to walk the entire length of the Dickey Ridge Trail, you'll need a pick-up at Compton Gap, Mile 10.4. Many people walk on the trail for a few miles, then retrace their steps.

If you are an Appalachian Trail hiker and plan to backpack the entire AT (or portions thereof) from north to south, you start at the Dickey Ridge Trail since it connects with the AT at Compton Gap.

The Dickey Ridge Trail begins in what was once an old pasture, which is now covered with new-growth trees and shrubs. After about 0.5 mile, there is a small stream, and you soon come to a left-hand side trail that leads to the entrance station on Skyline Drive. You quickly arrive at a bridge over the stream. For the next 0.75 mile or so, you can see stone walls, paths, and other remnants of old mountain homes.

Intervals: Vertical, 500 ft; Horizontal, 1 mi.

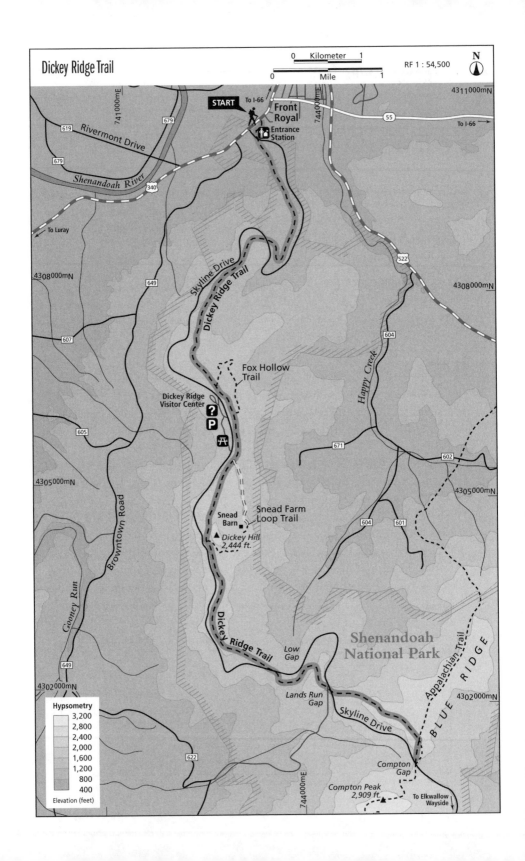

Soon the trail begins a rather steep ascent as it parallels the drive in its climb to Compton Gap. Along the way, you encounter the Dickey Ridge Visitor Center, the Fox Hollow Trail, and the Snead Farm Trail at mile 4.6. Low Gap is at mile 7.9, followed by Lands Run Gap at mile 9.2.

At the end of the Dickey Ridge Trail, a route of ascents and short descents, you encounter some beautiful views. The route crosses Skyline Drive several times. Rock hunters will delight in some of the geologic finds along the way.

The Dickey Ridge Trail joins the AT about 0.1 mile from Compton Gap. To complete the hike, turn right onto the AT and hike 0.1 mile to Compton Gap.

Miles and Directions

4.6 Junction with the Snead Farm Trail.

7.9 Low Gap.

9.2 Lands Run Gap.

10.3 Compton Gap.

2 Fox Hollow Trail

This short and easy loop makes a delightful history hike to an old homestead area. An interpretive pamphlet, available for a small fee at the Dickey Ridge Visitor Center, will enhance the hike. The trail is not rough and is suitable for children. Blue blazes mark the trail.

Skyline Mile: 4.6
Distance: 1.2 miles, loop.
Difficulty: Easy.
Traffic: Light to moderate.

Maps: National Geographic Trails Illustrated Topographic Map 228; Map 9, Appalachian Trail and Other Trails in Shenandoah National Park, North District (PATC, Inc.).

Finding the trailhead: This trail begins at the Dickey Ridge Visitor Center, Mile 4.6 on Skyline Drive, about 3 miles south of the Front Royal, Virginia, park entrance. Walk east across Skyline Drive to the park kiosk.

The Hike

The park kiosk provides further information about the area and serves as the trailhead. Pets are not allowed on this trail.

The trail begins with a slight descent and soon accesses Dickey Ridge Trail to the left. Turn left and follow that blue-blazed trail for 0.2 mile, then turn right (following the blue blazes) onto the Fox Hollow Trail. You will pass piles of rocks reflecting the

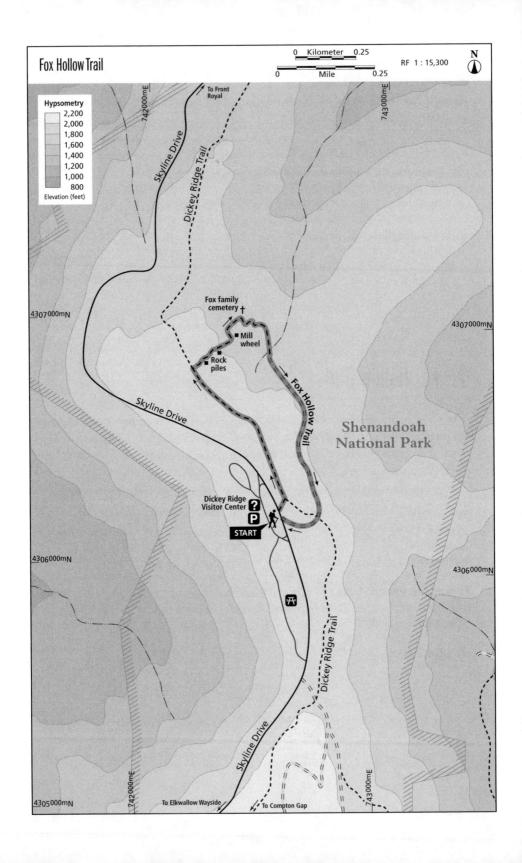

work once required to clear the forest and prepare it for cultivation.

Intervals: Vertical, 100 ft; Horizontal, .5 mi.

The trail continues to descend gradually, passing a spring and a mill wheel once used for ornamental purposes. At 0.5 mile the trail passes the Fox family cemetery. The largest stone memorializes Lemuel F. Fox, the son of Thomas Fox, who established the family farm here in 1856. According to the inscription, Lemuel died on May 24, 1916, at the age of 78. The trail continues to cross old pastureland now being reclaimed by the forest. Deer have returned to the area and now abound.

Shortly after passing the cemetery, the trail begins climbing gradually on its return to the visitor center. Along the trail, rock piles and rock fences continue to proclaim that farming once dominated the area. The path is actually an old road that once linked the Fox family with the town of Front Royal.

Upon completion of this short loop, you can extend your hike by following the description below (Hike 3: Snead Farm–Dickey Ridge Trail Loop).

Miles and Directions

100 yards Cement post. Turn left onto the blue-blazed Dickey Ridge Trail.

0.3 Cement post. Take right fork east onto the blue-blazed Fox Hollow Trail.

0.3 The first of many rock piles.

0.5 Fox family cemetery.

1.1 Cement post. Go straight to return to the visitor center.

1.2 Return to the trailhead, completing hike.

3 Snead Farm–Dickey Ridge Trail Loop

Appropriate for families, this hike takes you to buildings used by the Snead family when it homesteaded in the area.

Skyline Mile: 4.6
Distance: 1.4 miles out and back, or 3.2 miles, loop.
Difficulty: Shorter hike, easy; longer hike, moderately strenuous.

Traffic: Light to moderate.
Maps: National Geographic Trails Illustrated Topographic Map 228; Map 9, Appalachian Trail and Other Trails in Shenandoah National Park, North District (PATC, Inc.).

Finding the trailhead: Follow the directions in Hike 2 to the Dickey Ridge Visitor Center. Cross Skyline Drive to the east, opposite the exit for the Dickey Ridge Picnic Area. The trailhead can be accessed at the south end of the Fox Hollow Nature Trail Loop by turning left onto the Dickey Ridge Trail. The trail begins at Snead Farm Road, an old route with a chain gate, across Skyline Drive from the south end of the Dickey Ridge Picnic Area.

The Hike

Snead Farm was an active, privately owned operation until the 1950s. Today, its remnants are quite visible. The barn still stands, as does the root cellar. The stone remains of the Carter residence fill an open area. With a little imagination you can recognize the difficulty people had in clearing and farming this land.

After accessing the Snead Farm Road, bear left at the first fork, right at the second fork, and left at the last fork. The walk in to the farm is a pleasant one, since the road really is an old farm road. Upon reaching the farm, take time to explore the barn. Peer into the old root cellar; examine the stone foundation of the bunkhouse.

From Snead Farm, either retrace your steps to the picnic area for an out-and-back hike of 1.4 miles or continue a 3.2-mile loop hike by accessing the blue-blazed Snead Farm Loop Trail, which begins at a cement post near the bunkhouse foundation at mile 0.9.

Hike about 1 mile to another cement post at a T junction with the Dickey Ridge Trail. Go north (right) onto the Dickey Ridge Trail. The visitor center is 1.3 miles from this point.

The trail begins a slightly strenuous ascent to the top of Dickey Hill. At the summit, take the spur trail to your right. For a marvelous view of Signal Knob on Massanutten Mountain and

Intervals: Vertical, 200 ft; Horizontal, 1 mi.

The barn at Snead Farm.

the Shenandoah Valley, go left. A hang-glider launch area is located just before the path to the viewpoint.

Back on the Dickey Ridge Trail, make another quick ascent. The trail begins to descend gradually beneath a canopy of trees. It continues through a quiet woods to an intersection with Skyline Drive near the picnic area, thereby completing the loop.

Miles and Directions

- **0.1** Fork in road; stay left.
- **0.3** Fork in road; stay right.
- **0.5** Fork in road; stay left.
- **0.7** Remains of the Snead Farm. Retrace your steps for a hike of 1.4 miles. If continuing on the longer loop to return via the Dickey Ridge Trail, note the blue-blazed trail at the cement post opposite the stone ruins at mile 0.9. Follow this (the Snead Farm Loop Trail).
- **1.9** Cement post. Trail junction. Turn right onto the Dickey Ridge Trail.
- **3.2** Completion of loop. Return to the Dickey Ridge Visitor Center and Picnic Area.

Snead Farm–Dickey Ridge Trail Loop

0   Kilometer   0.25

0   Mile   0.25

RF 1 : 15,300

N

Hypsometry

2,600
2,400
2,200
2,000
1,800
1,600
1,400
1,200
1,000

Elevation (feet)

To Front Royal

Skyline Drive

Fox Hollow Trail

Dickey Ridge Visitor Center

4306000mN

4306000mN

742000mE

743000mE

START

Shenandoah National Park

Snead Farm Road

4305000mN

4305000mN

Dickey Ridge Trail

Skyline Drive

Signal Knob Overlook

Snead Farm Loop Trail

Root cellar

Snead Farm   Barn

Stone foundation

Cement post

Dickey Hill 2,444 ft.

Cement post

Snead Farm Loop Trail

4304000mN

4304000mN

742000mE

743000mE

To Mathews Arm

4 Lands Run Falls

An enjoyable jaunt down an old road leading to views of a pretty waterfall.

Skyline Mile: 9.2
Distance: 1.2 miles out and back.
Difficulty: Easy.
Traffic: Light to moderate.

Maps: National Geographic Trails Illustrated Topographic Map 228; Map 9, Appalachian Trail and Other Trails in Shenandoah National Park, North District (PATC, Inc.).

Finding the trailhead: The trail begins at the Lands Run parking area, Mile 9.2 on Skyline Drive, at the fire road on the south end of the parking lot.

The Hike

Three trails depart from the Lands Run parking area. The Dickey Ridge Trail crosses Skyline Drive at this point. It can be followed south for another 1.2 miles to its end at Compton Gap or taken north for 9.2 miles to the park entrance. Directly across the road from the parking area is the Hickerson Hollow Trail, a hike of 2.2 miles out and back, which goes through Hickerson Hollow (once the site of the mountain people's homes) and ends at the park boundary. The third trail is the Lands Run Falls Trail, which this narration describes.

Lands Run Falls is not especially high, nor can you see the entire falls from the trail, but the setting is lovely and the trek provides a nice leg stretch. The rocks leading out to a viewpoint can be treacherous, so use caution. Woods flanking the trail are dominated by oaks and hickories, interspersed with tulip poplars. Many of the healthiest oaks here were knocked down by a tropical storm in 1996; those not already denuded by gypsy moths were so heavily laden with leaves that they were easily toppled by the strong winds. In addition to a lovely forest, you will see a great deal of greenstone—volcanic rock exposed by soil erosion—on the uphill side of the road.

Follow the fire road, which descends immediately and continues to do so for 0.6 mile. At that point, a stream courses down the hill from the left and passes through a culvert under the road. The falls are on the right. By taking a short spur trail to the right, you can get some inspiring views. The slick rocks and precipitous grade create a potential hazard, so use caution.

The road continues for another 1.4 miles to the park boundary. Unless you

Intervals: Vertical, 50 ft; Horizontal, .20 mi.

have lots of energy to burn, there isn't much point in continuing the hike: The road descends another 600 feet with no viewpoints. Retrace your steps uphill from the falls.

Miles and Directions

0.6 Stream entering from the left goes under the road. Falls on the right. Retrace your steps after viewing the falls.

1.2 Lands Run parking lot.

Compton Gap Hikes (Skyline Mile 10.4)

Two short hikes—and several spur hikes from these primary hikes—depart from the Compton Gap area of Skyline Drive; all are detailed below. The area derives its name from the Compton family, after whom the gap and the peak to the west of the drive are named. The Comptons lived near Indian Run Spring, which can be easily accessed from a junction on the trail to Fort Windham Rocks.

Like other areas of the park, lands cut by these trails are also returning to a condition that will soon be a forest primeval. Huge chestnut trees, however, might not ever return, though saplings still grow along trails leading from the gap. Look for the characteristic elongated, pinnately compound leaves with serrated edges.

The area is rich in geology, and the trails course through boulder fields that derive from various geological origins. Lava once intruded into the area, and by investing only a little time you may come to appreciate the expansiveness of the lava flows and the changes that have occurred since these great volcanic outpourings. The Compton Peak Trail also offers views that can orient you to some of the main features in the North District.

5 Fort Windham Rocks–Indian Run Spring

A good leg stretcher offering photographic opportunities and insights into local geology.

Skyline Mile: 10.4
Distance: Fort Windham Rocks, 0.8 mile out and back or 1.6 miles with Indian Run Spring.
Difficulty: Easy.
Traffic: Light.

Maps: National Geographic Trails Illustrated Topographic Map 228; Map 9, Appalachian Trail and Other Trails in Shenandoah National Park, North District (PATC, Inc.).

Finding the trailhead: The hike begins at Compton Gap, Mile 10.4 on Skyline Drive. The trail begins on the fire road (which is also the Appalachian Trail) at the northeast end of the parking lot.

The Hike

Begin the hike by walking up the fire road (the Appalachian Trail) to a four-way junction. Turn left onto the Dickey Ridge Trail (blue blazes). The

Intervals: Vertical, 50 ft; Horizontal, .40 mi.

0   Kilometer   0.25

0   Mile   0.25

RF 1 : 15,300

N

4302000mN

To Lands Run Gap
and Dickey Ridge
VisiTor Center

Dickey Ridge Trail

Carson Mountain
2,580 ft.

To Lands Run Gap
and Dickey Ridge
Visitor Center

To park
boundary

746000mE

Shenandoah
National Park

Hypsometry

3,000
2,700
2,400
2,100
1,800
1,500

Elevation (feet)

Skyline Drive

Fort
Windham
Rocks

Appalachian Trail

Indian Run
Spring

Dickey
Ridge
Trail

Appalachian Trail

Indian Run

START

4301000mN

P

4301000mN

Compton
Gap

Skyline Drive

Indian Run
Overlook

CompTon Peak
2,909 ft.

Appalachian Trail

To
Jenkins
Gap

745000mE

746000mE

To Jenkins Gap, Mathews
Arm, and Elkwallow Wayside

path ascends gently through a new-growth forest that offers ideal habitat for ruffed grouse and other wildlife. Several broods dashed across the trail as we hiked toward the rocks.

As the trail levels, the 45- to 50-foot Fort Windham Rocks appear on your right. Geologists tell us the rocks are 600 to 800 million years old and are examples of the Catoctin lava formations. A short spur leads into the rocks.

On your return you might want to lengthen your hike at the cement post (the AT intersection) by dropping down the additional 0.2 mile to Indian Run Spring. The spring is off to your left and offers cool water, which should be filtered before drinking. From here, return to your vehicle.

Miles and Directions

0.2 Cement post, trail junction. Go left on the Dickey Ridge Trail to see the Fort Windham Rocks. Go right (downhill) to Indian Run Spring.

0.4 High rocks on right. Retrace your steps and return to the parking lot.

0.8 Parking lot.

6 Compton Peak

An out-and-back hike that follows the Appalachian Trail and climbs 835 feet to the summit of Compton Peak, where views are expansive and the geology intriguing.

Skyline Mile: 10.4
Distance: 2.4 miles out and back.
Difficulty: Moderate.
Traffic: Light.

Maps: National Geographic Trails Illustrated Topographic Map 228; Map 9, Appalachian Trail and Other Trails in Shenandoah National Park, North District (PATC, Inc.).

Finding the trailhead: The trail begins at Mile 10.4 on Skyline Drive across the road from the Compton Gap parking lot.

The Hike

The hike follows a mile-long segment of the Appalachian Trail, taking you to an intersection. Each fork of the intersection leads to a portion of Compton Peak, both of which are worth seeing. From the intersection, each knob is separated by a distance of only a few tenths of a mile.

The fork to the left proceeds a short distance, probably less than 0.1 mile, and then dips to an unexposed rock face. The face offers both foot and hand holds that you should probably use, particularly if the rocks are wet. The trail continues to a large boulder that stands roughly 18 feet high. Climb the boulder, for it offers great—on some days magical—views.

The view from the boulder also offers panoramas of the twin peaks of Mount Marshall and of Skyline Drive.

Return to the junction and hike to the other knob, only 0.2 mile round trip and easy to travel even if wet. This path soon crosses an almost indistinguishable crest that is Compton Peak and, almost as quickly,

Intervals: Vertical, 100 ft; Horizontal, .6 mi.

Compton Peak

0 Kilometer 0.25
0 Mile 0.25
RF 1 : 15,300

N

To Dickey Ridge
Visitor Center and
Lands Run Gap

To Hickerson
Hollow Trail

Skyline Drive

Appalachian Trail

Fort
Windham
Rocks

START

P

Compton
Gap

Shenandoah
National Park

Indian Run
Overlook

Appalachian Trail

Compton Peak
2,909 ft.

Appalachian Trail

Hypsometry
3,000
2,800
2,600
2,400
2,200
2,000
1,800
1,600
Elevation (feet)

Skyline Drive

To Jenkins Gap and
Mathews Arm

descends to a viewpoint. The picture before you includes views of the Piedmont Plateau and Dickey Ridge, which drops down toward Front Royal. Views from both these areas will help orient you to the country's surroundings.

Miles and Directions

0.2 Huge boulder on left side of the trail.

1.0 Cement post. Choose which knob of Compton Peak to see first.

1.4 Turnaround point after seeing both knobs.

2.4 Return to the trailhead.

7 Mount Marshall Trail and Beyond

A hike along three trails that highlight Shenandoah's beauty.

Skyline Mile: 12.35
Distance: 13.4 miles, loop.
Difficulty: Moderately strenuous to strenuous.
Traffic: Light.

Maps: National Geographic Trails Illustrated Topographic Map 228; Map 9, Appalachian Trail and Other Trails in Shenandoah National Park, North District (PATC, Inc.).

Finding the trailhead: The hike begins at the cement post in the parking lot at Mile 12.35 on the west side of Skyline Drive, 50 yards north of the Jenkins Gap Overlook. Follow the white-blazed Appalacian Trail south.

The Hike

The land around Marshall Mountain was once owned by John Marshall, who served as a county judge in the early 1800s.

Follow the Appalachian Trail south, which immediately begins a moderate climb through stands of striped maple taking over an old pasture. The trail is wide and easy on the feet because the ground is dirt rather than rock. In spring wildflowers are abundant. As the trail progresses, it levels, then descends toward Skyline Drive. Just before reaching the drive, there's an old Civilian Conservation Corps-built comfort station foundation on the left. It was never completed.

After 1.7 miles, the AT crosses the drive. Remain on the AT and ascend beneath a ceiling of red oak to North Marshall Mountain. The trail passes through Hogwallow Flat (2,745 feet), ideal deer habitat. As we hiked the area during the fall, we saw a number of white-tailed deer.

About 0.7 mile after crossing Skyline Drive, the AT comes to an obscure spring off to the left, bordered by rocks. The trail becomes rocky as it approaches the top of North Marshall (3,368 feet), reached after a sharp switchback. Trees obscure the view, but 0.1 mile later a spur trail leads to the right and provides lovely views to the west. On clear days you can see Browntown Valley. To the left are South Marshall, Hogback Mountain, Marys Rock, and Stony Man Mountain. To the right is Dickey Ridge. After a short descent, yet another spur trail leads to an even better overview.

The path becomes a brief, steep, and rocky descent but soon levels and widens as it reaches Skyline Drive at Mile 3.9. It's another 1.8 miles to the Bluff Trail. Continue on the AT south and begin ascending South Marshall Mountain, where the trail begins an easy ascent. The summit (3,212 feet) provides no views. Descend a short distance to a spur on the right, which takes you to a rock outcropping offering marvelous views to the west. On clear days, the landscape offers superb photographic opportunities.

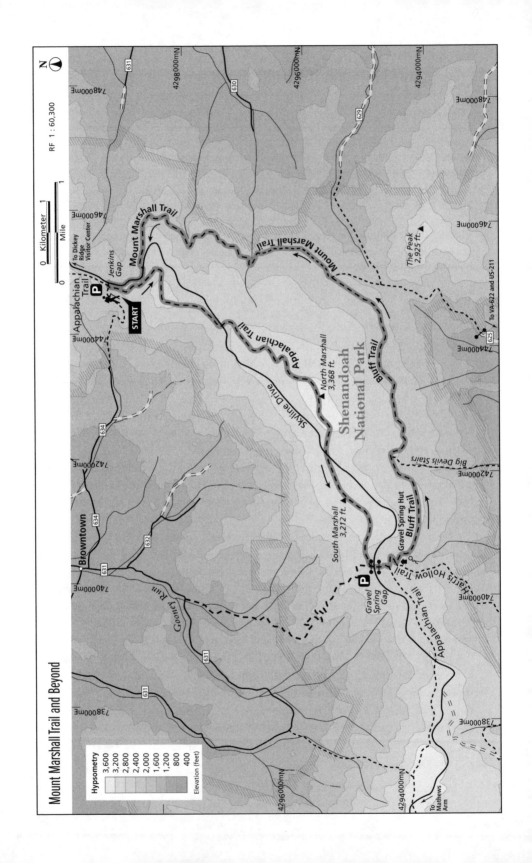

Mount Marshall Trail and Beyond

RF 1 : 60,300

N

0   Kilometer   1
0   Mile   1

Hypsometry
3,600
3,200
2,800
2,400
2,000
1,600
1,200
800
400
Elevation (feet)

631
630
629

4298000mN
4296000mN
4294000mN

748000mE
746000mE
744000mE

The Peak
2,925 ft.

To VA-622 and US-211

625

Mount Marshall Trail

Jenkins Gap

To Dickey Ridge Visitor Center

Appalachian Trail

P

START

Mount Marshall Trail

North Marshall
3,368 ft.

Appalachian Trail

Skyline Drive

Shenandoah National Park

Bluff Trail

Big Devils Stairs

South Marshall
3,212 ft.

Gravel Spring Hut

Bluff Trail

Harris Hollow Trail

Gravel Spring Gap

P

Appalachian Trail

Gooney Run

Browntown

634
634
632
631

631

To Mathews Arm

740000mE
742000mE
738000mE

4296000mN
4294000mN

The trail descends for nearly a mile to Skyline Drive and exits onto Gravel Spring Gap (2,655 feet). Cross the drive to the parking lot and join the AT at a cement post just south of the fire road. Continue about 0.3 mile through the woods to a cement post. Turn left onto the blue-blazed trail, which picks up the Bluff Trail in another 0.2 mile.

The path descends to a cement post by Gravel Spring. The Gravel Spring Hut is to your right. The area is delightful and provides an ideal spot for a lunch break. The hut is for day use only, unless you're a backpacker with a permit. From the spring, turn left.

Almost immediately, you see and take the yellow-blazed Bluff Trail to the right at a cement post. In 0.1 mile, pass a cement post and stay straight. Soon the trail makes a sharp switchback to the left at another cement post. Stay left on the Bluff Trail, which becomes a bit rough and rocky as it begins to ascend. Watch out for stinging nettles along the trail; the plants have deceptively beautiful white flowers in the fall. We saw lots of recent bear droppings on both the Bluff and Mount Marshall Trails.

At approximately mile 7.4, the Big Devils Stairs Trail merges from the right at a cement post and offers yet more adventure—and more distance—to this excursion. It makes an ideal hike of its own, and we offer it below as an alternative hike. This trail will add a mile to your trip.

The Bluff Trail proceeds straight. It is 2.3 miles to the Mount Marshall Trail along a rough, fairly level route. At mile 9.7 the trail encounters a cement post and its junction with the Mount Marshall Trail. Turn left, following the yellow blazes. Cross the four-branched Jordan River (here a small stream) almost immediately, and in about 1.1 miles cross another small creek—the Spruce Pine Branch. Throughout, you'll see many dead trees, the result of a gypsy moth infestation. At this point you're walking very near the park's eastern boundary.

The trail nears its end as you begin a descent along an old fire road. Soon the route crosses a third stream (Waterfall Branch), which is narrow with steep sides. After a short distance the trail ascends gently, offering brief views filtered by trees. Wild grape bushes line the trail. At the trail's end, turn right onto Skyline Drive, then walk past the overlook and north to the parking lot.

Alternative hikes: Three alternative hikes follow portions of the trail described above. The major difference is that the hikes can begin at different places along Skyline Drive. The Big Devils Stairs Trail begins from Mile 17.6—the Gravel Spring Gap parking lot. The Marshall Mountain hikes begin at the parking lot at Mile 15.95 (the Appalachian Trail crossing), at which point one hike is made by proceeding north, the other by proceeding south.

Alternative hike 7a: This strenuous 5.7-mile out-and-back excursion on the Big Devils Stairs Trail begins at the Gravel Spring Gap parking lot at Mile 17.6 on Skyline Drive and follows the same route as the more laborious Marshall Mountain hike. Follow the Appalachian Trail south (east of the drive). At 0.2 mile take the Bluff Trail to the left. After a 1.5-mile hike on the Bluff Trail, you reach a cement post. Turn right onto the Big Devils Stairs Trail, which stays on the north rim, offering inspiring views. We recommend turning around at the viewpoint.

Alternative hike 7b: Begin this easy hike on North Marshall Mountain at Mile 15.95 at the Appalachian Trail crossing. Proceed north on the AT (on the east side of the drive) from the parking lot. The hike is a short one, but it offers ideal wildlife habitat. The trail offers splendid views to the west, though not from the summit (see narrative above). It is approximately a 1.2 mile hike out and back to the summit, with a 300-foot elevation gain and loss.

Alternative hike 7c: This short, easy hike on South Marshall Mountain also begins from the parking lot at Mile 16 on the west side of the drive. It's about a 1.6-mile out-and-back trip to the rock viewpoint, 0.25 mile past the summit. This is a more confined view than the one from North Marshall, but it is still quite lovely. The elevation gain and loss is only 300 feet.

Miles and Directions

150 feet Cement post. Junction with the Appalachian Trail. Go south (left) on the AT, following white blazes. Ascend.

1.2 Trail levels. Begin descent.

1.7 Cement post at Skyline Drive. Cross the drive and continue south on the AT toward North Marshall Mountain.

2.4 A spring lies almost hidden on the left. At the same point, note the abundance of rocks placed on the path and around the trees.

3.0 Top of North Marshall. No views at summit due to trees.

3.9 Pass parking lot on the right and cross Skyline Drive to continue on the AT, south toward South Marshall Mountain.

4.5 Summit of South Marshall. Descend briefly for views.

5.4 Cement post at Gravel Spring Gap. Cross Skyline Drive, stay on the AT south (south end of lot). Do not access the yellow-blazed trail.

5.7 Cement post. Go left onto the blue-blazed trail that leads to the Bluff Trail in 0.2 mile.

Intervals: Vertical, 400 ft; Horizontal, 2 mi.

5.9 Cement post at Gravel Spring. Hut on right. Turn left and right, in quick succession. At the cement post turn onto the Bluff Trail (yellow blazes).

6.0 Cement post. The Harris Hollow Trail converges from the right. Stay straight and follow yellow blazes.

6.1 Cement post at switchback. Stay left on the Bluff Trail.

7.4 Cement post. Stay straight on the Bluff Trail or turn right for an additional 1-mile spur hike down and back on the blue-blazed Big Devils Stairs Trail.

9.7 Cement post at T. Turn left onto the Mount Marshall Trail (yellow blazes).

9.9 Cross Jordan River, a small four-branched stream. Low water in dry season.

11.0 Cross Spruce Pine Branch, a small stream.

11.9 Cross Waterfall Branch, a narrow stream with steep sides.

13.2 Skyline Drive. Go right, past the overlook.

13.4 End of loop. Return to your vehicle.

8 Keyser Run Fire Road–Little Devils Stairs Lariat

A beautiful hike, much of which is on a scenic fire road. The final portion climbs through a magnificent wild canyon and gorge.

Skyline Mile: 19.4
Distance: 7.5 miles, lariat.
Difficulty: Strenuous.
Traffic: Moderate.

Maps: National Geographic Trails Illustrated Topographic Map 228; Map 9, Appalachian Trail and Other Trails in Shenandoah National Park, North District (PATC, Inc.).

Finding the trailhead: From Skyline Drive, park at the Keyser Run Fire Road on the east side of the drive at Mile 19.4 and descend at the kiosk.

The Hike

The trail passes Bolen Cemetery toward the end of the fire road. The final part climbs through a magnificent wild canyon and gorge that requires boulder hopping and rock scrambling, so wear good boots. The rocks are slippery and dangerous when wet or icy, so use caution.

Walk 1 mile to reach Fourway Junction and a cement post. Continue straight on the fire road. The road descends into a large area of huge, sentinel-like trees that lend an aura of mystery to the woods.

At mile 3.3, the trail passes Bolen Cemetery on the left. A beautiful, peaceful place surrounded by a rock wall, the cemetery contains about forty-five gravestones. Just beyond the cemetery is a cement post. Turn left, still on the Keyser Run Fire Road, marked with a yellow blaze. Still descending, the road winds by remnants of

Bolen Cemetery on Keyser Run Fire Road.

old stone walls from the long-ago farming era. The route then passes near Pignut Mountain and a forest of pignut hickory trees.

Nearly a mile past the cemetery, the fire road ends at the park boundary as it meets Highway 614. Go around the chain and turn left, following the gravel road 0.1 mile to a parking lot. The trailhead for the Little Devils Stairs Trail is at the north end of the lot at a cement post.

Follow the blue-blazed trail, which immediately crosses Keyser Run in the form of two small streams. The trail begins a gentle ascent, winding as it passes through the woods. As views of Keyser Run open to the right, look to the far bank for a magnificent rock wall, a remnant of an old bridge. Traces of the road can be seen above the bridge wall, and without too much difficulty you can imagine the backbreaking work involved in clearing the rocks from the land and in building the various structures.

The trail becomes rocky, and it will only get worse! Look for the rock piles and walls scattered throughout the woods. We encountered a timber rattlesnake spanning the 4-foot-wide trail; it was in no hurry to move, but it finally crawled to the side, curled up under a fern, and, apparently, went to sleep.

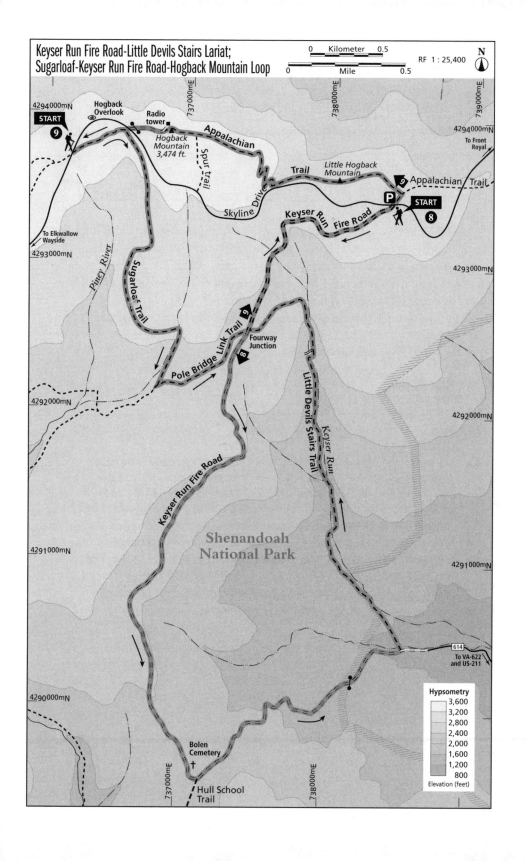

Keyser Run Fire Road-Little Devils Stairs Lariat;
Sugarloaf-Keyser Run Fire Road-Hogback Mountain Loop

Kilometer
0   0.5

Mile
0   0.5

RF 1 : 25,400

N

START
9

Hogback
Overlook

Radio
tower

Appalachian

Hogback
Mountain
3,474 ft.

Spur trail

Little Hogback
Mountain

Trail

Appalachian Trail

To Front
Royal

Skyline Drive

P

9

START
8

Keyser Run   Fire Road

To Elkwallow
Wayside

Piney River

Sugarloaf Trail

Pole Bridge Link Trail

9

Fourway
Junction

8

Little Devils Stairs Trail

Keyser Run

Keyser Run Fire Road

Shenandoah
National Park

614

To VA-622
and US-211

Bolen
Cemetery
†

Hull School
Trail

Hypsometry
3,600
3,200
2,800
2,400
2,000
1,600
1,200
800
Elevation (feet)

Intervals: Vertical, 500 ft; Horizontal, 1 mi.

After the rock walls, the trail begins a series of stream crossings. In summer the stream sometimes contains only a trickle. The rocky trail continues climbing and crisscrossing the water on boulders, which you must hop. The trail becomes quite steep, and there is more boulder hopping as the trail enters the ravine. Blue blazes on the trees and rocks guide you through the labyrinth.

At the top of the ravine, after a series of hard switchbacks, you finally emerge at Fourway Junction. At the cement post, turn right and ascend the Keyser Run Fire Road for 1 mile to return to your vehicle.

Miles and Directions

1.0 Fourway Junction. Continue straight on the fire road, descending.

3.3 Bolen Cemetery on left. Cement post just ahead. At cement post turn left, still descending on the fire road.

4.2 Park boundary. Come to gravel road (Highway 614). Turn left, descend to the parking lot. (Note: The hike begins here at the Little Devils Stairs Trail if accessed from outside of the park. Hike up the Little Devils Stairs Trail to Fourway Junction, turn left onto the Keyser Run Fire Road, follow it down past Bolen Cemetery, turn left onto the fire road to the park boundary and parking lot.)

4.4 At the end of the parking lot, turn onto the Little Devils Stairs Trail (blue blazes).

5.2 Begin more strenuous ascent, soon to enter ravine. Look carefully for blue blazes on trees and rocks.

6.5 Cement post at Fourway Junction. Turn right onto the Keyser Run Fire Road. Ascend.

7.5 End of lariat hike at the Keyser Run Fire Road parking lot.

9 Sugarloaf-Keyser Run Fire Road-Hogback Mountain Loop

A scenic trek providing spectacular views and an orientation to the area's geographical features.

See map on page 37.
Skyline Mile: 21.0
Distance: 4.9 miles, loop.
Difficulty: Easy to moderately strenuous.
Traffic: Light to moderate.

Maps: National Geographic Trails Illustrated Topographic Map 228; Map 9, Appalachian Trail and Other Trails in Shenandoah National Park, North District (PATC, Inc.).

Finding the trailhead: The hike begins just south of Hogback Overlook at Mile 21.0 on Skyline Drive. Park in the lot on the west (right) side of the drive. The Appalachian Trailhead is located at the south end of the parking lot at the cement post.

The Hike

Follow the AT north and descend 0.3 mile from the parking area to a cement post and turn right onto the blue-blazed Sugarloaf Trail. As the trail descends, mountain laurel lines the path. The woods are fairly open, and there is evidence of gypsy moth destruction. The country here is excellent bear habitat.

The trail crosses Piney Branch, a small stream, then passes several old stone walls. After 1.4 miles, the trail takes you to a cement post in a parklike setting. Go left onto the Pole Bridge Link Trail. In another 0.5 mile, you arrive at Fourway Junction. Turn left onto Keyser Run Fire Road and begin an easy ascent uphill for 1 mile. Cross the chain at the end of the fire road, then cross Skyline Drive onto the trail opposite you. You reach a cement post within 100 yards that directs you back onto the Appalachian Trail. Turn left onto the AT, ascend moderately for about 0.5 mile, after which the trail quickly takes you to a panorama on the right, just down from the top of Little Hogback Mountain. The views of the Shenandoah Valley, Massanutten Mountain, and way beyond are expansive.

From the rock overlook at the viewpoint, begin a descent. Do not access the spur trail, which soon comes in from the left and descends to Skyline Drive. Instead, stay right at the double white blaze. Descend into a dark wooded area under a heavy canopy of trees, then begin a 0.3-mile steep ascent with at least ten switchbacks to the first crest of Hogback Mountain. Some views can be had through the trees near the summit.

A cement post soon marks a left turn downhill to a spring; stay straight instead. Soon you'll come to a great view to the west. Browntown Valley lies below, and you can see how Massanutten Mountain splits the Shenandoah Valley. To the right lies

Dickey Ridge, and below it the town of Front Royal. This ledge and grassy area is one of three hang-glider launch sites in the park.

The short jaunt to the top of Hogback Mountain's second crest (3,474 feet) now begins as you head for the radio towers at the summit. This is the highest point in the park's North District. Descend toward Skyline Drive on the AT, which parallels and crosses the service road leading to the radio towers. Emerge on the drive. Cross the drive and, again, pick up the AT and follow it back to your vehicle to complete this hike.

Alternative hike 9a: For a shorter version, you can reach both Hogback Mountain and Little Hogback Mountain from just north of Hogback Overlook at Mile 20.8, where you will find an Appalachian Trail crossing and a service road. Park at the overlook or just south of it at the Mile 21.0 parking lot on the west. It's about a 0.5-mile out-and-back climb of 115 feet on the AT to the summit of Hogback Mountain and the views. A hike to Little Hogback Mountain and back from this point would add nearly 2 miles and so becomes a somewhat more strenuous hike. The views from both mountains are about the same (see descriptions above).

Miles and Directions

0.3 Cement post, turn right onto blue-blazed Sugarloaf Trail.

1.4 Cement post at T junction with the Piney Branch Trail. Go left onto the blue-blazed Pole Bridge Link Trail.

1.9 Cement post at Fourway Junction. Go left onto the Keyser Run Fire Road. The Little Devils Stairs Trail is straight ahead.

3.0 Leave the Keyser Run Fire Road. Cross Skyline Drive to trail directly opposite. Walk 100 yards to the Appalachian Trail and turn left.

3.5 Ascend to the summit of Little Hogback Mountain. View on right. Descend on the AT.

4.0 Spur trail. Do not follow spur left to the drive. Begin ascent to Hogback Mountain.

4.5 Cement post. Stay straight.

4.6 Hogback Mountain. Radio tower. Descend to the drive.

4.65 Cross the drive to the AT. Go right.

4.9 Parking lot. End of loop.

Intervals: Vertical, 200 ft; Horizontal, 1 mi.

10 Traces Trail

A forest hike along a trail that passes "traces" of mountain folk inhabitation and natural history.

Skyline Mile: 22.2
Distance: 1.7 miles, loop.
Difficulty: Easy.
Traffic: Moderate.

Maps: National Geographic Trails Illustrated Topographic Map 228; Map 9, Appalachian Trail and Other Trails in Shenandoah National Park, North District (PATC, Inc.).

Finding the trailhead: The hike begins at the east end of the amphitheater parking lot at the Mathews Arm Campground on Skyline Drive, Mile 22.2. Follow the blue blazes.

The Hike

This hike packs a lot into a short distance. It's a great route for a family with small children and for people with an interest in natural and cultural history. What's more, the trail is ideally located for RV campers since it departs from the Mathews Arm Campground. Dogs are prohibited on this trail.

As you hike on the Traces Trail, you'll see remnants of old rock walls, foundations, and roads. The hike is particularly pleasing in the fall when the leaves are red and gold. It's even pleasing when fog envelops the area and a light rain is falling. Whatever the conditions, don't pass this one up.

The trail is broad and begins beneath a mantle of red oak. Soon the trail climbs above the amphitheater. If the trail is wet, it may be slippery, so use caution. Toward the end of your hike, you come to a huge oak that for some reason was spared the ax. If trees could speak, this one could probably relate close to 200 years of history.

Near the trail's end, the forest canopy opens slightly, offering hints of other, more lofty vistas. After a 1.7-mile hike, you return via the trail to the west end of the parking lot.

Miles and Directions

0.4 Cement post at sign 9. Stay left, descend.

1.0 Cement post at sign 17. Go straight (sign 18 on left).

1.7 End of loop. Cross road to parking lot and vehicle.

Intervals: Vertical, 100 ft; Horizontal, .5 mi.

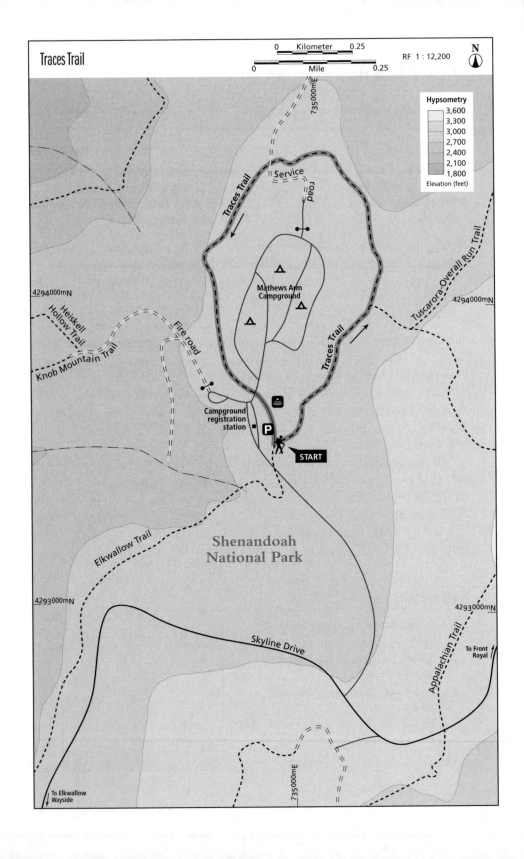

11 Tuscarora-Overall Run Trail Loop

A long hike, passing two beautiful waterfalls, with several very steep descents and ascents.

Skyline Mile: 22.2
Distance: 9.7 miles, loop.
Difficulty: Strenuous.
Traffic: Moderate.

Maps: National Geographic Trails Illustrated Topographic Map 228; Map 9, Appalachian Trail and Other Trails in Shenandoah National Park, North District (PATC, Inc.).

Finding the trailhead: The hike begins at Mile 22.2 on Skyline Drive at the amphitheater parking lot of Mathews Arm Campground.

The Hike

It's a good idea to be in shape and have lots of energy for this hike. The trail passes two beautiful waterfalls, but if the season has been a dry one, the falls could be reduced to merely a trickle. The trail also offers views of Massanutten Mountain and beyond. Note: On some older maps, the Tuscarora Trail used to be called the Big Blue Trail.

Begin this wilderness journey at the Mathews Arm Campground from the start of the Traces Trail. Follow the Traces Trail for about 0.4 mile to the first cement post. Stay on the trail (right) to the next cement post at interpretive sign 9. Go right and ascend to the next cement post. Turn left onto the Tuscarora-Overall Run Trail (blue blazes).

For the first 2 miles, the trail gently descends into Bear Wallow, where we saw lots of bear sign. The area is a bit swampy, with lots of tiny streams crossing the path. Rock piles dot the woods, and some blowdown flanks the trail. The route is a good one, although somewhat rocky.

Just before the trail begins a steeper descent to Upper Falls, you enter the designated wilderness. Prior to our hike, it had rained for three days, so the streams were full and both Upper Falls and Overall Run Falls were spectacular cascades. Soon after Overall Run Falls, you encounter a rock outcropping with a great panorama of Massanutten Mountain and beyond. Many hikers end their hikes here and retrace their steps, making a round-trip of between 4.5 and 5 miles.

The trail drops precipitously. Down in Overall Run, the trail levels but becomes incredibly rocky. Cactoctin greenstone is all around. Heading through the open woods, the route begins crossing Overall Run and does so quite often. For well over a mile, the path parallels the stream.

At a cement post at mile 4.6, stay left on the Overall Run Trail and leave the Tuscarora Trail, which goes to the right on its way out of the park. The main trail goes

Tuscarora-Overall Run Trail Loop

0　　Kilometer　0.75

0　　Mile　0.75

RF 1 : 41,700

N

To US-340

Overall-Beecher
Connecting Trail

Thompson
Hollow Trail

To VA-630 (parking
available at access)

Overall Run

Tuscarora Trail

Beecher Ridge Trail

East Fork

Heiskell Hollow Trail

Shenandoah
National Park

Tuscarora-Overall Run Trail

Mathews Arm
Campground

To Front
Royal

P

START

Elkwallow Trail

Appalachian Trail

Skyline Drive

To Jeremys
Run Trail

To Elkwallow
Wayside and
Thornton Gap

Hypsometry

| 3,600 |
| 3,200 |
| 2,800 |
| 2,400 |
| 2,000 |
| 1,600 |
| 1,200 |
| 800 |
| 400 |

Elevation (feet)

4297000mN
4296000mN
4295000mN
4294000mN
4293000mN
733000mE
734000mE
735000mE
736000mE

straight and descends under a canopy of trees. Soon the trail widens on what was once an old road. Then it swings a bit away from the run.

At mile 5.2, at a cement post and a double blue blaze, keep left onto the Overall-Beecher Connecting Trail. (The Overall Run Trail once went straight here, leading to the park boundary, but it's abandoned.) Cross the run twice and begin a very steep ascent of the ridge, still on the Overall-Beecher Trail.

At the next cement post turn left onto the yellow-blazed Beecher Ridge Trail. Descend briefly, then begin a moderate ascent. At mile 6.6 turn right onto the Heiskell Hollow Trail. The trail soon descends steeply. Cross the stream two times and come to a cement post. Here, the Heiskell Hollow Trail goes both directions; turn left for this hike. Then it ascends and ascends and ascends for at least 1.7 miles to a cement post at a T intersection. Go right, still on the Heiskell Hollow Trail,

Intervals: Vertical, 500 ft; Horizontal, 1 mi.

still climbing the rocky path. This continues for another 0.8 mile until arriving at a junction with a service road. Go left onto the road and follow it 0.5 mile back to your vehicle and the end of the loop hike.

This is a long hike with a series of steep ascents and descents. But don't cut this one short—it's a beautiful hike. Not many people hike past the falls, so if you're seeking solitude and a good workout, go for it.

Miles and Directions

0.4 Cement post. Stay to right on the Traces Trail. Go 50 feet to another cement post at interpretive sign 9. Turn right, uphill.

0.6 Cement post. Turn left onto the Tuscarora (formerly Big Blue)-Overall Run Trail (blue blazes).

0.7 Huge boulder on left (greenstone).

1.1 Pass through the swampy Bear Wallow. Trail fairly level.

2.2 Cement post (three-way junction). Stay straight on the Tuscarora-Overall Run Trail for about 70 yards to another cement post. Turn left, still on the Tuscarora-Overall Run Trail.

3.1 Bottom of Overall Run.

4.6 Cement post. Stay left on the Overall Run Trail (the Tuscarora Trail now branches off to right).

5.2 Cement post. Go left onto the Overall-Beecher Connecting Trail (blue blazes).

5.8 Cement post. Turn left onto the Beecher Ridge Trail (yellow blazes) in order to access in another 0.8 mile the Heiskell Hollow Trail.

6.6 Cement post. Turn right onto the Heiskell Hollow Trail and ascend.

8.4 Cement post. Turn left on the Heiskell Hollow Trail, still ascending.

9.2 Cement post at T at service road. Turn left onto road, follow it to chain, cross chain, make short walk to parking lot.

9.7 Amphitheater parking lot. End of loop.

12 Thornton River

Thornton River is a loop hike that descends through some of the park's best bear country. It passes artifacts of the mountain people and meanders along one of the park's most beautiful streams.

Skyline Mile: 24.0
Distance: 10.6 miles, loop.
Difficulty: Strenuous.
Traffic: Light.

Maps: National Geographic Trails Illustrated Topographic Map 228; Map 9, Appalachian Trail and Other Trails in Shenandoah National Park, North District (PATC, Inc.).

Finding the trailhead: The hike begins at Mile 24.0 at the parking lot of Elkwallow Wayside on the west side of Skyline Drive.

The Hike

The Thornton River is named after Francis Thornton, who bought land around 1740 and built a mansion, Montpelier, which still stands. Many other Shenandoah place names honor him, including F. T. Valley and Thornton Gap.

Begin the hike from the Elkwallow Wayside. From the parking lot, take the Appalachian Trail north and follow it across Skyline Drive. Follow the trail uphill for about 1 mile. At mile 1, you encounter a cement post. Turn right and proceed along this trail for only a few yards to another cement post. Turn right onto the Piney Ridge Trail. The left branch is short and leads to the Range View Cabin, operated by the Potomac Appalachian Trail Club (PATC) and available on a reservation basis (see Appendix A: For More Information and Appendix D: Where to Stay).

Shortly after the cement post, a metal tag on a tree reads BLISTER RUST CONTROL AREA. Blister rust is a disease produced by a spore that attacks white pine trees. Like many diseases, it can be devastating and has wiped out entire forests of white pine. Blister rust control was a major resource protection project in the park in the early 1960s.

At mile 3, the Piney Ridge Trail intersects the Fork Mountain Trail. Bear right. The trail continues to drop. At mile 3.5 there are magnificent stands of tulip poplar. At mile 4.2 you encounter another cement post. Turn right onto the Hull School Trail, an old road that winds down and crosses several tiny streams.

At mile 4.9 stands another cement post, at the access to the Thornton River Trail. Turn right, past a number of rock piles. Within a mile, the trail crosses the North Fork of the Thornton River four times in rapid succession. When we hiked this trail, fall leaves, patches of fog, and deer in the mist gave the river a sublime mood.

At 5.4 miles the trail crosses the Thornton River again. The trail is flanked by a rock wall. The trail then swings widely and climbs to a broad ridge forested with red

Intervals: Vertical, 500 ft; Horizontal, 2 mi.

oak. You will find an old rock structure here, perhaps an old chimney. In places, old strands of barbed wire litter the ground. The trail continues a gradual climb.

At mile 6.3 the trail returns to Skyline Drive. Cross the drive and walk left for about 100 yards to where you find the continuation of the Thornton River Trail. Climb the trail for about 0.25 mile, where you'll quickly pick up the AT; turn right (north). The AT parallels Skyline Drive and returns you back to Elkwallow Wayside.

Miles and Directions

1.0   Cement post. Turn right onto the Piney Ridge Trail.

1.01 Another cement post almost immediately after mile 1. Turn right onto the Piney Ridge Trail.

1.8   Dense pinewood forest.

3.0   Cement post and intersection with the Fork Mountain Trail. Stay straight onto the Fork Mountain Trail; the Piney Ridge Trail goes north (left).

3.5   Beautiful (magnificent) stands of tulip poplar.

4.2   Cement post. Turn right onto the Hull School Trail.

4.9   Cement post at junction where the Hull School Trail intersects with the Thornton River Trail. Turn right onto the Thornton River Trail.

5.4   Fourth crossing over the Thornton River.

5.6   Artifacts of mountain folks.

6.3   Cement post at Skyline Drive. Cross Skyline Drive and hike left along the drive.

6.4   Spur trail to the Appalachian Trail.

6.7   Cement post. Turn right onto the AT.

9.1   Cement post and intersection of the AT with beginning of the Jeremys Run Trail. Turn right, still on the AT.

10.6 Return to vehicle.

13 Knob Mountain–Jeremys Run Lariat

A full-day hike into the wilderness surrounding Jeremys Run.

Skyline Mile: 24.1
Distance: 12.6 miles, lariat.
Difficulty: Strenuous.
Traffic: Moderate.

Maps: National Geographic Trails Illustrated Topographic Map 228; Map 9, Appalachian Trail and Other Trails in Shenandoah National Park, North District (PATC, Inc.).

Finding the trailhead: The hike begins at the lower end of Elkwallow Picnic Area parking lot, just south of the Elkwallow Wayside at Mile 24.0 on the west side of Skyline Drive. Walk down the trail and immediately access the Appalachian Trail (white blaze).

The Hike

If you are a wilderness buff, this one's for you. You could also make this a backpacking trip, camping at the bottom of Jeremys Run. The trails meander through the designated wilderness areas of Knob Mountain and Jeremys Run. There is a great view from Knob Mountain, and this hike is a long, beautiful trek into the heart of Shenandoah National Park.

Begin by descending south on the Appalachian Trail at the brown signpost at the bottom level of the Elkwallow Picnic Area. Lush grasses line the trail in this forest of tall trees. Soon the path winds by a water pipe on the left.

After about 0.3 mile, you encounter a cement post. Stay straight on the Jeremys Run Trail (blue blazes). Descend through a mature, open forest of oaks and maple—the squirrels love it here!

Descend to a cement post at a three-way junction and turn right onto the Knob Mountain Cutoff Trail (blue blazes). The trail descends, crosses Jeremys Run, then immediately begins to ascend. There is definitely a wilderness feeling to the area, but even so the trail is a good one. Continue the ascent, which is steep in parts and contains many switchbacks. After passing a long rock wall (which bisects the trail at a double blue blaze), a cement post indicates a junction with the Knob Mountain Trail (yellow blazes). Turn left onto the Knob Mountain Trail. From this point, it's about 3 miles to the summit along what is actually an old road.

You are now on a nice, soft ridgetop trail. Soon the trail begins a steady uphill climb offering occasional views through the partially open forest. When we hiked Shenandoah, grouse populations were high, providing food for an assortment of predators. On this hike, we came across a huge pile of grouse feathers as if someone had just plucked the bird. A bobcat may have taken the bird, though owls also prey on grouse.

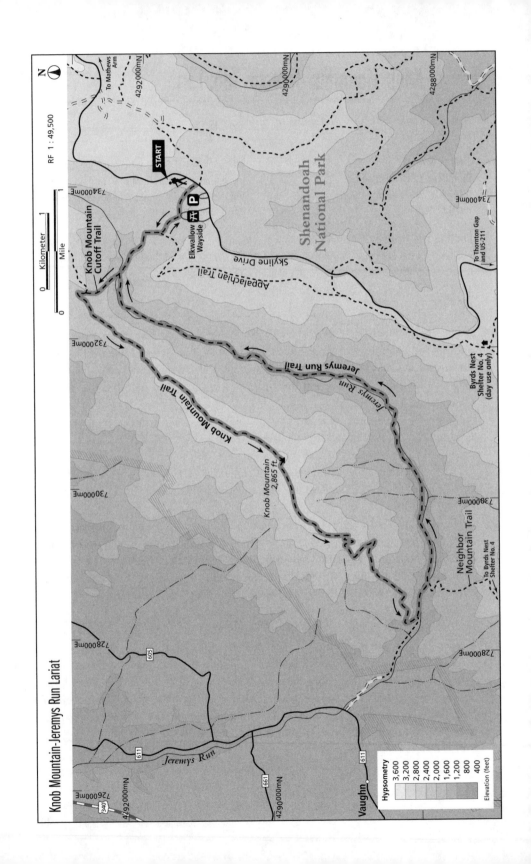

Knob Mountain-Jeremys Run Lariat

Not long before the summit of Knob Mountain (2,865 feet), the old road narrows, ends, and becomes a trail once more. There is a cement post just before the top that indicates you have 250 more steep feet to go.

Stay straight (there's no other way) and begin a descent that will drop you 1,600 feet in the next 2.4 miles. The descent begins immediately, at first dropping very steeply through a series of sharp switchbacks. Then the drop becomes much more gradual along a good, soft trail. Views begin to open to the south and southwest into Jeremys Run and to Neighbor Mountain across the run. On an October day when leaves are in full color, the view would be spectacular.

The path keeps descending until it begins to parallel Jeremys Run, on the right. Almost immediately the trail ends by a wood marker on this side of the run. At this point you cross the run for the first (but not nearly the last) time. Look for a yellow blaze on a tree on the other side, as well as a cement post situated right after the crossing. Turn left to another cement post 45 feet away at a fork. Take the left fork onto the Jeremys Run Trail (blue blazes); the right fork is the Neighbor Mountain Trail.

Sycamore trees grow along Jeremys Run, but many were knocked down by the high winds and heavy flooding of 1995.

The next run crossing comes very soon, and the trail (a good one) winds slightly upward. Piles of rocks are abundant in the woods, and even though there isn't much of a water flow in dry seasons, the setting is pretty.

The third crossing occurs suddenly, so watch carefully for the blue blazes. The areas here and just ahead offer some possible backcountry camping spots. Look carefully and be sure to abide by backcountry regulations.

The next 4-plus miles negotiate a series of stream crossings with an ascent so gradual that it is hardly noticeable. At approximately mile 11.8, you'll see another cement post. Continue straight and ascend more steeply for another 0.5 mile. The AT comes in here. Stay straight and follow the AT north for the last 0.3 mile to complete the loop at the picnic area parking lot.

Intervals: Vertical, 500 ft; Horizontal, 2 mi.

Miles and Directions

1.6 Cement post. Turn left onto the Knob Mountain Trail (yellow blazes), an old fire road.

3.8 Begin to ascend summit. The road becomes a trail.

4.6 Reach summit (2,865 feet). Cement post. No views at summit. Begin descent of approximately 1,600 feet to Jeremys Run.

7.0 At wood post, ford Jeremys Run for the first time. Look for yellow blaze on tree across run. Cement post. Turn left for 45 feet to another cement post at a fork. Stay left onto the Jeremys Run Trail (blue blazes). The right fork leads to Neighbor Mountain.

11.8 Cement post. Stay straight, following blue blazes.

12.3 Cement post and junction with the Appalachian Trail. Take the AT north, staying straight (white blazes).

12.6 Picnic grounds, parking lot, and end of hike.

14 Byrds Nest Summit and Byrds Nest Shelter No. 4

A fun hike up to one of four day-use shelters in the park, through a deciduous forest. A tranquil hike.

Skyline Mile: 28.5
Distance: 2.8 miles out and back
Difficulty: Easy to moderate.
Traffic: Light.

Maps: National Geographic Trails Illustrated Topographic Map 228; Map 9, Appalachian Trail and Other Trails in Shenandoah National Park, North District (PATC, Inc.).

Finding the trailhead: The trail begins at the Beahms Gap parking area, Mile 28.5 on Skyline Drive. The trailhead is located at a cement post at the north end of the parking lot.

The Hike

This short, relatively easy day hike takes you up to a ridge on the Neighbor Mountain Trail and to the Byrds Nest Shelter No. 4, a day-use shelter built in 1965. It is one of four shelters in the park constructed with donations from former Sen. Harry F. Byrd Sr. The trek is pretty and tranquil. On clear days you can see beyond Pass Mountain to the east. Once there were views from the shelter, but trees have obscured most of them. The shelter is a large, three-sided stone structure with a huge fireplace and a picnic table.

Begin this hike at the cement post at the north end of the parking lot. Descend 0.1 mile through the woods to a T junction at another cement post. Here the Appalachian Trail runs north/south. Turn north (right) onto the AT. Soon you'll encounter a cement post indicating a spring on the left.

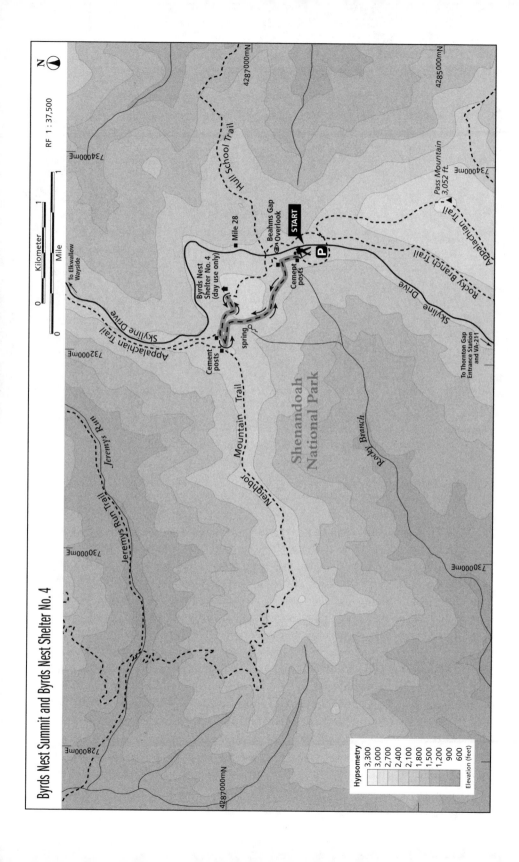

Byrds Nest Summit and Byrds Nest Shelter No. 4

RF 1 : 37,500

N

Kilometer

Mile

Hypsometry

3,300
3,000
2,700
2,400
2,100
1,800
1,500
1,200
900
600

Elevation (feet)

To Elkwallow Wayside

Appalachian Trail

Skyline Drive

Jeremys Run

Jeremys Run Trail

Cement posts

spring

Byrds Nest Shelter No. 4 (day use only)

Mile 28

Hull School Trail

Beahms Gap Overlook

START

Cement posts

P

Neighbor Mountain Trail

Shenandoah National Park

Rocky Branch

Rocky Branch Trail

Skyline Drive

Appalachian Trail

Pass Mountain 3,052 ft.

To Thornton Gap Entrance Station and VA-211

Byrds Nest Shelter No. 4.

As you trek through a mostly deciduous forest (pretty in the fall), the trees and rocks offset one another's beauty. There are a few short, steep ascents and a few very rocky areas of trail. Sturdy boots are recommended, especially if the trail is wet.

At 0.8 mile you will reach Byrds Nest Summit. Here you'll encounter a four-way junction of the AT and the Neighbor Mountain Trail. Turn east (right) onto the Neighbor Mountain Trail. In 0.1 mile another post is encountered. Here, stay straight on the Neighbor Mountain Trail for 0.5 mile more to Byrds Nest Shelter No. 4.

You'll find the shelter in a pretty setting, one that inspires a picnic. A field lies in front of you and flowers give color in the summer. Pass Mountain rises to the east. If you wander to the right above the shelter, it may be possible to get some views, but nothing outstanding. From here, you'll need to retrace your route to the parking lot. You will note that in the first 0.6 mile of the return trip, at the cement posts, you are able to take a short spur trail down to Skyline Drive. If you do make this choice, be aware that you will come out north of where you left your vehicle at Beahms Gap.

If you are in the mood for only a very short walk in the forest, a loop walk of only 0.4 mile, try this: Access the cement post at the north end of the parking lot.

Intervals: Vertical, 100 ft; Horizontal, .20 mi.

Go 0.1 mile to another cement post at a T, which is the AT intersection. Go left (south) on the AT, following the blue blazes on the trees. Soon you ascend briefly and return to Skyline Drive, beside the parking lot.

Miles and Directions

0.0 Cement post, north end of parking lot at Beahms Gap.

0.1 Cement post and junction with the Appalachian Trail. Turn north (right) onto the AT.

0.2 Spring on left; stay on AT.

0.8 Byrds Nest Summit. Four-way cement post. Turn right onto the Neighbor Mountain Trail.

0.9 Another cement post; stay straight on Neighbor Mountain Trail.

1.3 Cement post; stay straight on Neighbor Mountain Trail.

1.4 Byrds Nest Shelter No. 4. Retrace your steps back to parking lot.

2.8 Beahms Gap parking lot.

Central District
Skyline Mile 31.6 to 65.5

Some of the park's roughest and tallest peaks are in the Central District. These include Old Rag, the park's most formidable and spectacular mountain, and Hawksbill, the park's highest mountain (4,050 feet).

With the exception of Old Rag, which requires special directions, access to the Central District is most easily made by taking U.S. Highway 33 from Stanardsville or Harrisonburg and entering Shenandoah National Park at Swift Run Gap. From the north, take U.S. Highway 211 from either Sperryville to the east or Luray to the west and access the park at Thornton Gap.

The Central District's Lewis Spring Falls ▶
tumbles more than 80 feet.

Central District Overview

0 Kilometers 3
0 Miles 3

RF 1 : 228,000

N

To Front Royal
Luray
211
Park Headquarters
To Elkwallow Wayside
Thornton Gap Entrance Station
Panorama
17
211
To Sperryville
18
19
15
340
Shenandoah River
211
BUS 340
20
340
Shenandoah River
21
22
Stanley
Skyland
23
611
24
26
Shenandoah
National
25
16
27
Park
Big Meadows
Byrd Visitor Center
?
32
28
To US-522
29 30 31
600
33
643
670
600
231
Skyline Drive
670
649
34
662
Lewis Mountain
615
35
662
36
665
37
Madison
38
Swift Run Gap Entrance Station
33
29
230
Stanardsville
810
To Loft Mountain

Hypsometry
5,000
4,000
3,000
2,000
1,000
0
Elevation (feet)

15 Pine Hill Gap-Broad Hollow Loop

A hike along a trail often overgrown with much vegetation but which provides, toward the trail's end, glimpses of a bygone era.

Skyline Mile: 31.5
Distance: 5.8 miles, loop.
Difficulty: Moderate.
Traffic: Light.

Maps: National Geographic Trails Illustrated Topographic Map 228; Map 10, Appalachian Trail and Other Trails in Shenandoah National Park, Central District (PATC, Inc.).

Finding the trailhead: From the park, depart at Mile 31.5 at Thornton Gap on Skyline Drive. Take U.S. Highway 211 east to Sperryville, Virginia. From Sperryville continue on US 211, picking up U.S. Highway 522 south. Go 0.8 mile, turn right onto Highway 231 and go 3.3 miles. Just before the bridge over the Hazel River, take Highway 681, a dirt and gravel road, west past Highway 600 (Highway 600 enters from the right after 1 mile). Continue on Highway 681 for a total of 2.5 miles, where you encounter a cement post at the top of a left bend in the road immediately adjacent to a private road. Park well to the right of the private drive in the spot that can accommodate one or two cars. You'll return here along the Broad Hollow Trail, which this post designates. Hike Highway 681 to the road's end, then climb a poorly maintained road that parallels the park boundary.

The Hike

Trails in this part of Shenandoah are remote and difficult. On the other hand, these trails wander through some of the park's best examples of artifacts from a bygone era. On this particular trail, you'll encounter remains of old cabins. Remember that some sections of the trail are falling into disuse, and you might need to allocate more time than you would for other trails of a comparable distance. In some places, the vegetation is so thick that it almost blots out the sky overhead.

After parking your vehicle in a very restrictive space (two small cars, maximum), follow the key points carefully. The trail follows Highway 681 to its terminus, then follows an old road.

At mile 2.2 the Pine Hill Gap Trail joins with the Hazel Mountain Trail, which you must follow. At mile 2.5 your trail intersects with the Hot-Short Mountain Trail from the west, and you continue on the Hazel Mountain Trail. At mile 3.5, turn right onto the Sams Ridge Trail, which soon crosses a small stream. Just 0.1 mile later, turn right onto the Broad Hollow Trail. At mile 4.4 you encounter a cabin on your immediate left. Just 0.2 mile later, cross a stream, which may in fact be part of the trail. Keep your eyes open for a roofless cabin, then two old cabins and several stone walls. At mile 5.2 the trail crosses a stream, only to recross the same stream again, and at mile 5.8 yet again. Now climb the short bank to return to your vehicle.

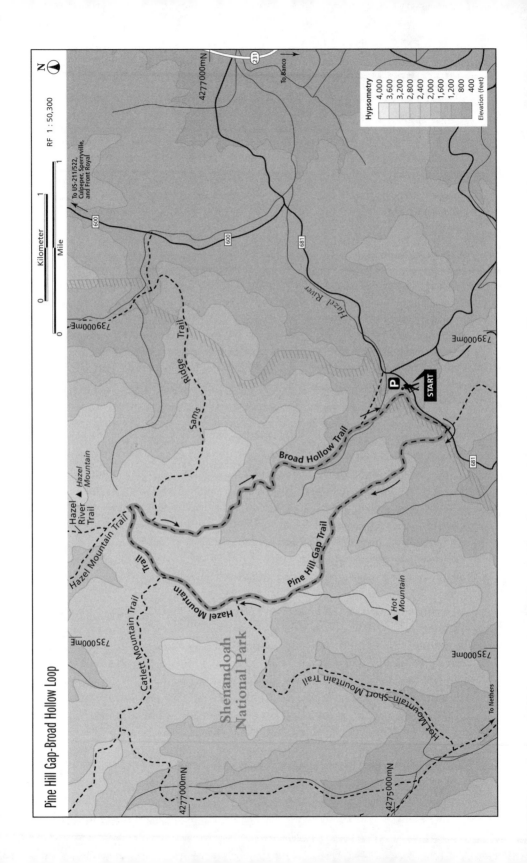

Pine Hill Gap-Broad Hollow Loop

RF 1 : 50,300

Kilometer

Mile

Hypsometry

4,000
3,600
3,200
2,800
2,400
2,000
1,600
1,200
800
400
Elevation (feet)

To US-211/522,
Culpeper, Sperryville,
and Front Royal

600

600

681

231

To Banco

4277000mN

739000mE

Hazel River

START

P

Broad Hollow Trail

Sams Ridge Trail

Hazel River Trail

Hazel Mountain ▲ Hazel Mountain

Hazel Mountain Trail

Catlett Mountain Trail

735000mE

Hazel Mountain Trail

Pine Hill Gap Trail

Hot Mountain ▲ Hot Mountain

681

Shenandoah National Park

Hot Mountain–Short Mountain Trail

To Nethers

4277000mN

4275000mN

735000mE

Intervals: Vertical, 500 ft; Horizontal, 1 mi.

Miles and Directions

0.5 Cement post and access to the Pine Hill Gap Trail. Climb steadily on the Pine Hill Gap Trail.

2.2 Cement post. Junction and join with the Hazel Mountain Trail. Continue straight, now on the Hazel Mountain Trail, still climbing.

2.5 Cement post marking access for the Hot-Short Mountain Trail to the west. Continue climbing on the Hazel Mountain Trail.

3.5 Turn right to access Sams Ridge Trail.

3.6 Cross small stream.

3.7 Turn right onto the Broad Hollow Trail and remain on this trail until hike's end.

4.4 Pass the cabin on the trail's immediate left.

4.6 Cross the stream, which for 15 yards or so is actually part of the trail, depending on the weather.

4.8 To the trail's right 30 feet sits an old roofless cabin overgrown with vines and squeezed by maturing trees.

5.0 Off the trail 50 yards sit two old cabins and several stone walls.

5.2 Cross stream. Trail levels but continues slow descent.

5.4 Cross stream again, which is now on the right.

5.8 Cross stream, climb short bank, and access vehicle.

16 Old Rag

A climb to the top of one of the park's most famous peaks, with incredible views from the summit.

Skyline Mile: 31.5
Distance: 5.6 miles, to summit and back, or 7.2 miles to continue on loop. (Add 1.6 miles to these totals if you park in the lower lot.)
Difficulty: Strenuous.

Traffic: Moderate to heavy (especially on weekends and holidays).
Maps: National Geographic Trails Illustrated Topographic Map 228; Map 10, Appalachian Trail and Other Trails in Shenandoah National Park, Central District (PATC, Inc.).

Finding the trailhead: The most popular and easiest way to climb Old Rag is to access the trailhead from outside the park. We recommend using a good road map, such as the *Virginia Altas and Gazetteer.* If you're in the North District of the park, from Mile 31.5 at Thornton Gap on Skyline Drive, take U.S. Highway 211 8 miles east to Sperryville, Virginia. From Sperryville on US 211, turn onto U.S. Highway 522 south. Go 0.8 mile, turn right onto Highway 231, and go 8 miles. Turn right onto Highway 601. In 0.3 mile turn right at a T intersection. Continue on Highway 601 until it becomes Highway 707 some 0.8 mile later. In 1.7 miles the road becomes Highway 600 (bearing left); follow it for 0.5 mile to the parking lot on the left, which is clearly marked. From here you must walk 0.8 mile to the trailhead at the terminus of Highway 600. On very uncrowded days, try driving up Highway 600 to the small parking lot at the trailhead, but it fills rapidly.

From the south (Charlottesville, Virginia) take U.S. Highway 29 about 35 miles north to Madison, Virginia. From Madison, take Highway 231 north for 12.8 miles. Turn left onto Highway 602. In 0.5 mile the road becomes Highway 601. Continue on Highway 601. In 0.8 mile it becomes Highway 707, and it becomes Highway 600 1.7 miles later. Follow Highway 600 for 0.5 mile to the parking area on the left. Access the blue-blazed Ridge Trail.

The Hike

The rocks of Old Rag are among the park's oldest. Billions of years ago, the granite that forms the crest of Old Rag was thousands of feet underground. With time, the rocks uplifted to the point where they now perch atop this 3,268-foot mountain. At the same time, the igneous rock that once surrounded today's boulders eroded and exposed them. Seeing these rocks shrouded in all the various weather conditions is one of the rewards of hiking to the summit of Old Rag. Another reward includes completing a quick self-taught course in "Rock Climbing 101" as you scramble over and under boulders. Just be sure not to climb on days when the rocks are wet. No pets are allowed on the Ridge Trail or the Saddle Trail.

Because of Old Rag's popularity, the Park Service has implemented a management plan. As part of that plan it suggests you consider climbing Old Rag on

Rocks atop Old Rag.

weekdays, particularly during the popular fall hiking season. Overuse has already created abuse of the mountain, and hikers parking on private property have caused some ill feelings among local landowners. Presently the park is working with landowners to improve its strategy so that all may enjoy this area.

If the parking lots are full, do not park on nearby private property but drive elsewhere for an alternative hike. The park also recommends that hiking groups carpool and not send out groups by the busload.

The National Park Service enforces strict parking regulations at the trailhead. Anyone over 16 without a seven-day pass, a yearly pass, or a Golden Eagle or Golden Age pass must buy a $5.00 permit. Such permits are available from park personnel on busy weekends and holidays or by self-registration at the trailhead. If you plan to stay in the backcountry, obtain a free backcountry permit from one of the visitor centers. The park prohibits camping at elevations more than 2,800 feet on Old Rag. Nor is camping permitted near Byrds Nest Shelter No 1. Byrds Nest Shelter No. 1 and the Old Rag Shelter are for day use only, but hikers may camp at least 100 yards from the Old Rag Shelter.

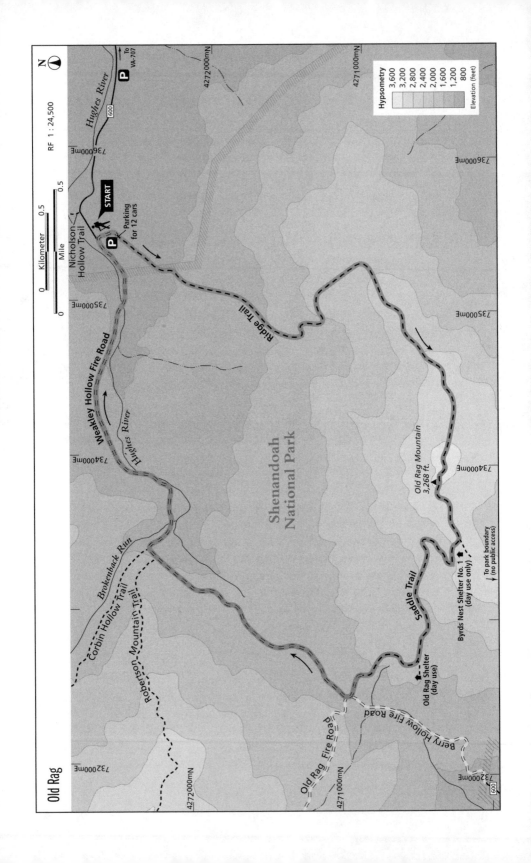

Old Rag

RF 1 : 24,500

Kilometer
0   0.5
Mile
0   0.5   0.5

N

To VA-707

Hughes River

600

START

Parking for 12 cars

Nicholson Hollow Trail

Weakley Hollow Fire Road

Hughes River

Ridge Trail

Brokenback Run

Corbin Hollow Trail

Robertson Mountain Trail

Shenandoah National Park

Saddle Trail

Old Rag Mountain 3,268 ft.

Byrds Nest Shelter No. 1 (day use only)

To park boundary (no public access)

Old Rag Shelter (day use)

Old Rag Fire Road

Berry Hollow Fire Road

600

4272000mN

4271000mN

4271000mN

4272000mN

732000mE

732000mE

734000mE

734000mE

735000mE

735000mE

736000mE

736000mE

Hypsometry
3,600
3,200
2,800
2,400
2,000
1,600
1,200
800
Elevation (feet)

Byrds Nest Shelter No. 1.

If crowds are minimal and the two lots open, you may begin your hike from either the lower or the upper parking lot. During crowded periods, you'll have to begin from the lower lot as the upper one—0.8 mile away—will be full.

From the trailhead proper, the hike begins by progressing along the Ridge Trail. During the first 0.75 mile the trail is wide, then it begins to get narrow and rocky. About 1 mile along the trail, huge boulders appear through the forest, hinting at what lies ahead. A small stream that is about sole deep greets you in July; in spring the stream may be a torrent. The forest canopy soon opens, offering a view of a nearby mountain range. About 1.5 miles along the trail, the vegetation closes in. A short distance later, the hike stops and the crawl begins.

For about 1 mile or more, you must shinny over boulders using, in places, three-point stands. Those who have mastered elementary rock-climbing techniques have an advantage. Some, however, may be alarmed by the heights, and one man we encountered decided to turn back. He was smart, for he knew his limits. Others have slipped and fallen, and some have broken bones. Yet others, such as Senator Byrd, have made annual climbs of Old Rag even at advanced ages—meaning into their late seventies! Regardless, the going is slow and requires a while to navigate the labyrinth of rocks. The route is well marked with blue blazes, and without them finding the route could be exceedingly difficult. Pay attention to the blazes; after reaching one, look for the next before proceeding.

Though the trail becomes more obvious after threading through the maze, another maze soon follows. Fortunately, this one is much easier to negotiate. Shortly after the second maze, you reach the summit of 3,268-foot Old Rag. The summit is marked by a cement post. Go past it on the right to get the full effect of the views. From the summit, you have the option of either retracing your steps or following the longer but easier route back to your car. Timewise, it is probably a toss-up, but remember, if you return by the same route, you must scramble down the boulders and, for most, this is more difficult than climbing up.

We returned by the longer route, leaving from the summit of Old Rag and proceeding 0.4 mile down to Byrds Nest Shelter No. 1. Another mile and we reached the Old Rag Shelter. From there the trail continues downhill. At mile 4.6—about 0.4 mile past the shelter—turn right onto the Weakley Hollow Fire Road at the cement post marked OLD RAG PARKING. The fire road is level; finally, it parallels the Hughes River. Just before reaching the upper parking lot, the trail crosses three footbridges over the river. As you reach the fourth footbridge 0.1 mile beyond the other three, you're nearly at the upper parking lot. If your vehicle is in the lower lot, there is 0.8 mile left to this hike.

Alternative hike 16a: To embark on a trek from Skyline Drive for an out-and-back hike of approximately 14 miles, park on the east side of Skyline Drive at Mile 43.0 and access the Old Rag Fire Road. Stay on the fire road, going east/southeast for about 5 miles to the Old Rag Shelter. Along the way, you cross the Whiteoak Canyon Trail, the Limberlost Trail, and the Skyland Horse Trail, and about 0.5 mile before the shelter, you cross the intersection of Berry Hollow and Weakley Hollow Fire Roads.

Camping is permitted at least 100 yards from of the fire shelter. From here, it's about 1.4 miles farther to the summit of Old Rag, reached by taking the Saddle Trail

Intervals: Vertical, 500 ft; Horizontal, 1 mi.

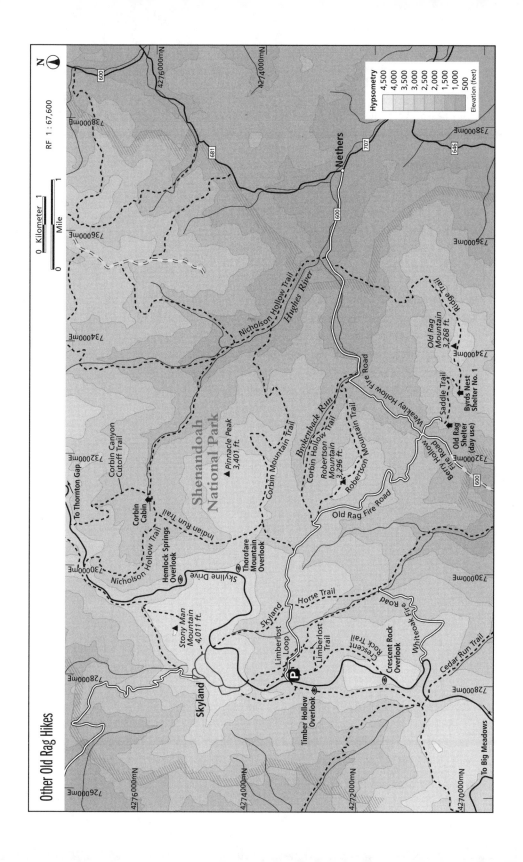

Other Old Rag Hikes

from the Old Rag Shelter. From the summit, retrace your steps for a total hike of about 14 miles, out and back. Ideally, you'll want to make this a three-day trek.

There are yet other Old Rag hikes, and we suggest you study a good topo map for all the varying trails to and from Old Rag. We have not described all the possible routes here, merely the ones we believe might be best.

Miles and Directions

1.5   Top of ridge—out of the trees and into the rocks.

2.8   Summit of Old Rag. Descend at cement post following the Saddle Trail.

3.3   Byrds Nest Shelter No. 1. Turn right.

4.2   Old Rag Shelter and spring. Continue on the Saddle Trail/fire road.

4.6   Double junction. Turn right onto the Weakley Hollow Fire Road at cement post marked OLD RAG PARKING.

5.7   Cement post. Stay straight. The Robertson Mountain Trail comes in from the left.

5.8   Cement post. Stay straight. The Corbin Hollow Trail comes in from the left.

6.0   Cross a metal footbridge.

7.0   Cross three consecutive wooden footbridges.

7.1   Cross a fourth wooden footbridge.

7.2   Parking lot at end of Highway 600. End of loop hike.

17 Marys Rock

Appropriate for families, this hike offers natural history, geology, panoramic views, and folklore.

Skyline Mile: 31.6
Distance: 3.6 miles out and back.
Difficulty: Easy to moderate.
Traffic: Moderate.

Maps: National Geographic Trails Illustrated Topographic Map 228; Map 10, Appalachian Trail and Other Trails in Shenandoah National Park, Central District (PATC, Inc.).

Finding the trailhead: The trail begins at the Panorama upper parking lot, Mile 31.6 on Skyline Drive.

The Hike

If you have the luxury of time, pick a clear day for this hike and go early in the morning. Sunrise is a great time to enjoy the views and get some superb photos. (Save foggy days for hikes to waterfalls; fog adds to the aura of wetness.)

According to one version of park lore, a young woman named Mary Thornton once made this hike alone to the rocky summit. When she returned, she carried a bear cub under each arm. The Park Service certainly does not endorse such intimacy with wildlife today, but the story is a good one.

To begin the trek, head left (south) on the Appalachian Trail, which is marked with white blazes. Within 30 yards, the trail begins to climb. Twelve log steps help you upward. Within 100 yards, five more log steps do the same thing. The trail winds upward through a hardwood forest interspersed with mountain laurel and ferns. It follows the east side of the ridge. Soon the trees are more widely spaced and views begin. The trail becomes very rocky and is fortified on your left with a man-made shelf of rocks. On the upward slope, the trees seem to be trying to restrain the force of gravity, preventing large boulders from tumbling down the hillside. The ascent is steady, with some switchbacks and few level areas.

After about a mile, you can see large rock monoliths on your right and a lovely panorama to the east. As you approach the summit, the trail swings back into the trees. On the uphill side of the trail, thick stands of mountain laurel line the path. At our approach, a ruffed grouse took wing.

Watch for the first cement post after 1.7 miles. Do not turn left onto

Intervals: Vertical, 400 ft; Horizontal, .5 mi.

0   Kilometer 0.5

0   Mile   0.5

RF 1 : 34,900

N

To Elkwallow Wayside

To Panorama
and Luray

Thornton
Gap

Thornton Gap
Entrance Station

17
START

4282000mN

Shenandoah
National Park

Thornton

P

211

To
Sperryville

Marys Rock
3,514 ft.

Appalachian Trail

Skyline Drive

SKINNER RIDGE

Buck Hollow Trail

Hollow

Buck

River

Beech Spring Hollow

BUCK RIDGE

Buck Ridge Trail

START
18 19

Meadow
Spring Trail

P
18

18

19

19

Hazel Mountain Trail

WHITE ROCKS

White Rocks Trail

4280000mN

Cave

Hazel River

Hazel
River Trail

734000mE

736000mE

Hazel
Mountain
Trail

To
Skyland

Hypsometry

	3,600
	3,200
	2,800
	2,400
	2,000
	1,600
	1,200
	800

Elevation (feet)

the AT. Continue straight ahead, taking the spur trail to the top, which is 0.1 mile
farther. Be sure to follow the blue blazes, not the white ones along the AT.

Marys Rock is composed of Pedlar granodiorite. The vista below is wonderful;
you can see Thornton Gap. Plan to spend some time resting in the clearing or carefully climbing the rocks for different views. You may see peregrine falcons soaring
on the wind drafts, as we did.

Now that you've climbed 1,210 feet to the top, you can enjoy the luxury of a
downhill return. Backtrack, taking the AT north, but use caution: The steep, rocky
descent can be more hazardous than the uphill trek, especially when wet.

◀ *Trail to Marys Rock.*

Miles and Directions

0.1 Junction with the Appalachian Trail. Turn left.

1.0 Large rock monoliths on right.

1.7 Cement post. Go straight on spur trail. Do not turn left on the AT.

1.8 Summit of Marys Rock. Turnaround point.

3.6 Upper parking lot at Panorama.

18 Buck Hollow-Buck Ridge Trail Loop

An invigorating loop hike along a rushing stream that descends through a hollow, then climbs Buck Ridge. The trail leads to a rarely visited, wild section of the park.

See map on page 71.
Skyline Mile: 33.5
Distance: 5.6 miles, loop.
Difficulty: Moderately strenuous.
Traffic: Light.

Maps: National Geographic Trails Illustrated Topographic Map 228; Map 10, Appalachian Trail and Other Trails in Shenandoah National Park, Central District (PATC, Inc.).

Finding the trailhead: The trail begins at Mile 33.5 on Skyline Drive at the south end of the Meadow Spring parking area. Stay left on the Buck Hollow Trail and descend.

The Hike

Within 0.1 mile the trail approaches a stream, which comes in from the right. The stream is only a small trickle, but within 0.7 mile its volume increases, and then at 1 mile from the trailhead it cascades over a series of rock tiers. The trail remains steep and continues its descent into Buck Hollow.

At 2.8 miles from the trailhead, the Buck Hollow Trail joins the Buck Ridge Trail. The Buck Ridge Trail goes right at a metal tag on a cement post. The Hazel Mountain Trail is 2.3 miles away and Skyline Drive is 2.8 miles away.

Intervals: Vertical, 500 ft; Horizontal, 1 mi.

From the junction, the Buck Ridge Trail begins a gradual descent that is deceiving. Within 0.1 mile the trail begins its ascent of sixty-some log steps. Though it seems forever, the trail tops out at the stairs in about 0.1 mile, a brutally steep section.

In early July, and along this particular exposure, the laurel has all gone to seed, but what a sight this is in late spring. Blueberry and huckleberry bushes also abound, and bears feed on them in late summer and early fall. Also along the trail are an abundance of Indian pipes, a saprophyte that is pure white when it first emerges.

Toward the end of the trail, still along Buck Ridge, the trail approaches a boulder field. Most of the rocks are lichen covered. With time, these elementary plants play a vital role in the creation of soils. Again, the trail cuts sharply into the ridge, then ascends. Several tenths of a mile later the trail levels, but only briefly. It again begins a gradual ascent, where it follows a rounded yet exposed ridge. A bit farther, the ridge merges with other hills. To the right climbs Skinner Ridge; to the left stands Hazel Mountain. Woods flanking the trail offer excellent wildlife habitat. On the hike we heard a woodpecker and saw several white-tailed deer. At mile 5.1 you reach a trail junction with the Hazel Mountain Trail. Turn right and return to the parking lot, completing your journey in 0.5 mile for a total of 5.6 miles.

Miles and Directions

0.7 Trail swings right. Cross stream on rocks.

1.8 Trail swings right, crosses small stream, then swings hard left and crosses wider part of stream. Avoid old road.

2.7 Cross main Buck Hollow stream.

2.8 Cement post, trail junction. Take hard right onto the Buck Ridge Trail. Cross stream and begin ascending steeply.

3.9 Views of Thornton Gap.

5.1 The Hazel Mountain Trail comes in on the left. Bear right, still on the Buck Ridge Trail.

5.6 Parking lot and end of loop hike.

19 Hazel Falls and Cave

A four- to five-hour hike that provides views of a small but spectacular falls with the added feature of a lovely cave.

See map on page 71.
Skyline Mile: 33.5
Distance: 5.4 miles out and back.
Difficulty: Relatively easy except for last 0.2 mile, which is very steep.
Traffic: Moderate.

Maps: National Geographic, Illustrated Topographic Map 228; park handout map. Map 10, Appalachian Trail and Other Trails in Shenandoah National Park, Central District (PATC, Inc.).

Finding the trailhead: The trail begins at Mile 33.5 on Skyline Drive at the south end of the Meadow Spring parking area. Stay left on the Buck Hollow Trail and descend.

The Hike

Though not a high drop, Hazel Falls is impressive as it snakes down a mountain-side, pausing long enough to create several tranquil pools. In the fall when leaves variegated with reds, yellows, and oranges dot these pools, the falls have an added charm. Looking upstream, several caves flank the run to the right, and because of their size, the mind can have fun conjuring up the different uses people and various species of wildlife have invariably made of them through the years.

The trail to Hazel Falls and Cave begins with a large Park Service interpretive sign located a few yards from the trailhead that recounts the recent history of fire in the area. According to the sign, the Big Run Fire of 1986 burned 4,475 acres, while the Calvary Rocks Fire burned 1,431 acres in 1998. The sign further points out that the largest fire in Shenandoah began in the Pinnacles Picnic Area on October 29, 2000. Another fire was discovered on Old Rag Mountain the next day. By the time the fires were contained, more than 24,000 acres had burned. The sign is worth studying, as you will soon see some of the devastating effects of several of the fires as you hike toward Hazel Falls. In fact, fires downed so much timber that in sections, trail crews dropped many hazardous snags to protect hikers on days when high winds often topple snags. You'll see the remaining stumps and downed snags, for there are many.

The trail is relatively flat and a generally easy hike. At mile 2.5 you'll reach the only difficult part of the hike. Though steep, the last 0.2 mile is straight down, but the short distance means your suffering will be brief—both down and up. But despite the brevity, don't underestimate the down portion. Sometimes we find that those with "football knees" have more trouble going down than they do going up—even if they're otherwise in tremendous shape. Well-placed flat rocks facilitate the descent—and ascent—to and from the falls.

Upon reaching the first small pool, enjoy and then proceed up and along the right side of the stream. Within about 30 yards you'll come to one of the area's caves. The other cave is located high among the rocks and will require some scrambling and some searching. This cave is much larger and can be most easily accessed from the pool you first reached following that 0.2-mile descent.

The return to the trailhead is generally up, so factor in more time than

◀ *Hazel Falls and Cave.*

what you needed for your trip down. Because of the area's general beauty and the amount of time you'll probably spend at the various pools and caves, we believe you may need a total of about five hours, particularly if you're a photographer.

Miles and Directions

0.0 Meadow Spring parking lot; access the Hazel Mountain Trail.

0.5 The Buck Ridge Trail comes in from the left. Stay right (east) on Hazel Mountain Trail.

1.6 The White Rocks Trail comes in from left. Take this trail.

2.5 Signpost indicating that the cave/falls is 0.2 mile downhill, making a sharp right.

2.7 Falls and, about 100 yards upstream on the right, a cave. Other caves are in the area but require some looking.

5.4 Meadow Spring Parking Lot.

20 Corbin Cabin Cutoff-Nicholson Hollow-Appalachian Trail Loop

A five- to six-hour, 4.2-mile hike that provides glimpses of the bygone era of the mountain people.

Skyline Mile: 37.9
Distance: 4.2 miles, loop.
Difficulty: Moderately strenuous.
Traffic: Moderate.

Maps: National Geographic Trails Illustrated Topographic Map 228; Map 10, Appalachian Trail and Other Trails in Shenandoah National Park, Central District (PATC, Inc.).

Finding the trailhead: Park at Mile 37.9 on the west side of Skyline Drive. The trailhead is at a cement post (cross at the north end of the parking lot). Access the Corbin Cabin Cutoff Trail here and travel east.

The Hike

This loop trail descends on the Corbin Cabin Cutoff Trail and ascends via the Nicholson Hollow Trail and, on the other side of Skyline Drive, ends by way of the Appalachian Trail. The trail passes "Freestate" Hollow and an abandoned cabin.

Corbin Cabin and other artifacts from mountain families provide a legacy of a bygone era. Put in other words, hiking the trail provides a glimpse of what life may have been like for the men, women, and their families who lived in the hollows.

George Corbin lived and farmed near the head of the Hughes River, raised his family, and, like many others, left the area when Congress created Shenandoah National Park. Oral history testimony recalls that Corbin borrowed $500 to remodel the cabin and to add a metal roof. Today, the place must look very much like the home Corbin originally built in 1910 when he was twenty-one. The small, cozy

Nicholson Cabin on the Corbin Cabin Cutoff Trail.

place is separated into two sections, one for cooking and lounging, the other for sleeping, and it can be rented from the Potomac Appalachian Trail Club (see Appendix A: For More Information).

Corbin Cabin perches on a bank of the Hughes River. On the other bank, about 100 yards to the west, another cabin apparently served as the home of John T. Nicholson, an in-law of Corbin. That cabin, however, is slowly melting into the forest of pine, oak, and maple.

Other artifacts of a bygone era also exist, most of which you'll discover if you take the time. If you're interested in the area's history, take a look around; this is not an area to rush through.

Appropriately, the hike begins by descending a trail built by the mountain people who once inhabited the area. Begin at the trailhead on the east side of Skyline Drive and drop gradually for about 25 yards to a cement post that identifies the 1.4-mile hike to the Corbin Cabin.

As the trail continues to drop, you are flanked on either side by lush stands of mountain laurel. The trail is steep and rocky. After about 0.5 mile, it turns to the right in a southeasterly direction. To your east is a small, dry streambed. Shortly thereafter, the trail levels and begins to climb gradually.

Corbin Cabin Cutoff-Nicholson Hollow-
Appalachian Trail Loop

0   Kilometer   0.25

0   Mile   0.25

RF 1 : 15,300

N

To Thornton Gap

Appalachian Trail

Appalachian Trail

P

START

Skyline Drive

Appalachian Trail

Hughes River Gap

Appalachian Trail

Stony Man Overlook

To Skyland

4277000mN

730000mE

731000mE

Shenandoah National Park

Corbin Cabin Cutoff Trail

Nicholson Cabin

Nicholson Hollow Trail

4276000mN

Hughes River

To park boundary

PATC Corbin Cabin

Nicholson Hollow Trail

Indian Run Trail

Hemlock Springs Overlook

Skyline Drive

730000mE

731000mE

To Skyland

4275000mN

Hypsometry

3,900
3,600
3,300
3,000
2,700
2,400
2,100
1,800

Elevation (feet)

Intervals: Vertical, 200 ft; Horizontal, 1 mi.

About 0.9 mile from the trailhead you encounter the first clear remnants of early human activity. Jumbles of rocks flank the right side of the trail, and to the left, downhill, are the ruins of the John R. Nicholson Cabin. The flowing stream below it has a nice pool.

Continue on the trail to the Corbin Cabin. Just before rock hopping across the Hughes River, you see another cabin that once belonged to Albert and Mamie Nicholson. It is hidden in the trees to the right of the trail. This one is fairly intact, allowing you to get an idea of how it was constructed.

The Corbin Cabin is in front of you as you cross the river. The Potomac Appalachian Trail Club (PATC) renovated it in 1954 and now rents it to hikers. The spot is idyllic, and you may want to have a picnic in the yard if no one is currently renting.

At this point, you must make a choice. Do you retrace your steps, for a hike of 2.9 miles? Or do you return via the somewhat steep Nicholson Hollow Trail and add another 1.4 miles to your route?

If you choose to continue on the loop hike, return to the cement post below the Corbin Cabin and take the old mountain road that leads west (left). This is the Nicholson Hollow Trail, which ascends (steeply in places) to Skyline Drive. The first part of the trail is extremely rough and rocky as it crosses Indian Run (often dry) and climbs through the forest. More than a mile from the cabin, you'll encounter a walled-in spring on the left side of the trail, but it is usually dry.

The upper portion of the Nicholson Hollow Trail is a fairly straight climb to Skyline Drive. The path is flanked by mountain laurel and lots of oak.

Upon reaching the drive, turn left and walk south for about 75 yards. Cross the drive to your right at an opening in the trees and continue straight ahead to access the AT at a cement post. Turn north (right) onto the AT. Follow it as it winds up and down, until you reach the parking area, thus completing this scenic loop.

Miles and Directions

0.5 The Corbin Cabin Cutoff Trail goes left, then right to parallel a streambed.

0.9 Stone wall on right. John R. Nicholson Cabin ruins downhill to left.

1.4 John T. Nicholson cabin in woods to right of trail.

1.45 Hughes River crossing. Cement post below Corbin Cabin.

1.58 Junction with the Indian Run Trail. Keep straight.

1.8 Indian Run stream crossing (often dry).

2.9 Enclosed spring on left.

3.8 Skyline Drive. Turn south onto the drive, cross drive to cement post. Turn north onto the Appalachian Trail.

4.2 Follow the AT to trailhead and vehicle.

21 Stony Man Trail

An interpretive trail to the peak of Stony Man Mountain.

Skyline Mile: 41.7
Distance: 1.4 miles lariat.
Difficulty: Easy.
Traffic: Moderate to heavy.

Maps: National Geographic Trails Illustrated Topographic Map 228; Map 10, Appalachian Trail and Other Trails in Shenandoah National Park, Central District (PATC, Inc.).

Finding the trailhead: At the north entrance of Skyland—a complex that includes a lodge, restaurant, and riding stable—at Mile 41.7, park just inside at the Stony Man Nature Trail lot. At the cement post, access the Appalachian Trail north.

The Hike

At 4,011 feet, Stony Man is the park's second-highest mountain after Hawksbill. The park provides a brochure for this interpretive hike, which includes twenty stops. Pets are not allowed on this trail.

From the Stony Man parking area inside Skyland, access the Appalachian Trail at the cement post. Follow the trail north (right) for 0.4 mile. Here, the AT reaches its highest point in Shenandoah. At this point, the trail continues straight at the intersection for 0.1 mile to a split in the trail. Either fork will take you to the summit, because the two actually meet to form a loop. At the summit, take time, particularly in the spring, to search the sky for falcons. Over the years, the National Park Service has sponsored a peregrine reintroduction program intended to restore the nation's fastest-diving bird to the wild. This program, also embraced by the state of Virginia, took place from 1989–1993 and from 2000–2005 in Shenandoah.

Intervals: Vertical, 50 ft; Horizontal, .5 mi.

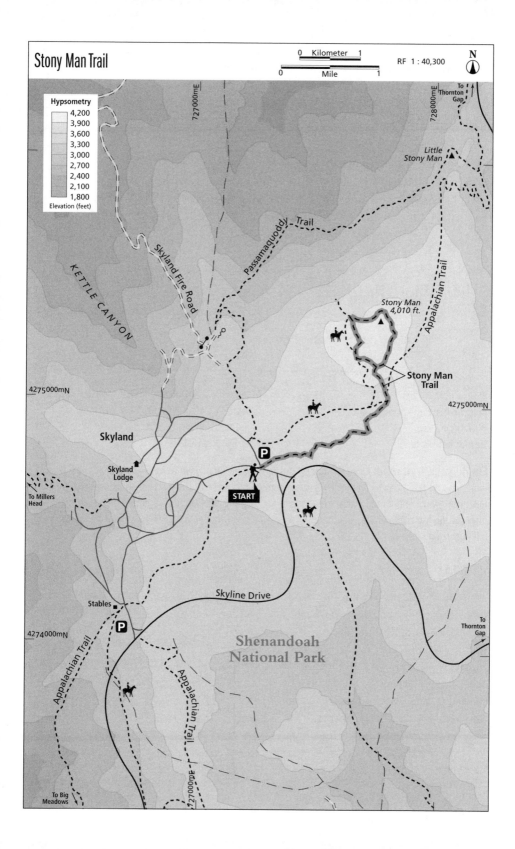

Stony Man Trail

0 Kilometer 1
0 Mile 1

RF 1 : 40,300

N

Hypsometry

	4,200
	3,900
	3,600
	3,300
	3,000
	2,700
	2,400
	2,100
	1,800

Elevation (feet)

727000mE

728000mE

To Thornton Gap

Little Stony Man

KETTLE CANYON

Skyland Fire Road

Passamaquoddy Trail

Stony Man 4,010 ft.

Appalachian Trail

4275000mN

Stony Man Trail

4275000mN

Skyland

Skyland Lodge

To Millers Head

START

Stables

Skyline Drive

Shenandoah National Park

Appalachian Trail

To Thornton Gap

4274000mN

Appalachian Trail

727000mE

To Big Meadows

To complete the hike, continue around the loop and back to the AT. You're on familiar ground; return the way you came.

Miles and Directions

0.0 From trailhead, take AT north.

0.4 Junction at cement post with the Stony Man Nature Trail. Go straight on blue-blazed trail.

0.5 Fork in trail. Stay right.

0.7 Summit of Stony Man, cement post, and junction. Right or left forms loop to viewpoint.

1.0 Cement post and junction with the Appalachian Trail. Head straight south on the AT.

1.4 Stony Man parking lot.

22 Millers Head

A short hike starting from the Skyland complex to an observation platform with delightful views.

Skyline Mile: 42.5
Distance: 1.6 miles out and back.
Difficulty: Easy.
Traffic: Moderate.

Maps: National Geographic Trails Illustrated Topographic Map 228; Map 10, Appalachian Trail and Other Trails in Shenandoah National Park, Central District (PATC, Inc.).

Finding the trailhead: From the north, turn right off Skyline Drive at Mile 42.5, the south entrance into the Skyland complex. Pass the stables on your left. The road forks; follow the left fork. Soon you'll encounter a gravel road; turn in and park. Walk about 75 yards up the paved road (to the top of Bushytop Mountain) to a cement post indicating the Millers Head Trail. Turn left (west) onto the trail.

The Hike

You can actually begin your hike in one of two ways. You can walk up the gravel road from your car for 0.2 mile to the Millers Head Trail on the left, or you can walk up the paved road to the cement post. Either way, you walk to the top of Bushytop Mountain. There you see some large microwave dishes, part of the Skyland communication system.

Once on the Millers Head Trail, head downhill via a series of switchbacks. About 0.3 mile before the obser-

Millers Head

0 Kilometer 0.25
0 Mile 0.25
RF 1 : 15,300

N

727000mE

KETTLE CANYON

Skyland Fire Road

4275000mN

Hang-glider launch area
Millers Head
Observation platform

Millers Head Trail

To Stony Man and Thornton Gap

P North entrance

Skyland
START
Skyland Lodge

To Thornton Gap

Bushytop

728000mE

Shenandoah National Park

Appalachian Trail

Skyline Drive

Stables

Hypsometry
4,200
3,900
3,600
3,300
3,000
2,700
2,400
2,100
1,800
Elevation (feet)

P

4274000mN

728000mE

To Pollock Knob
To Big Meadows

vation platform, you encounter a cement post. Keep going down the trail to the platform. Along the way, you will have some good views, but none are as nice as the one from the Millers Head observation platform at an elevation of about 3,460 feet. From here, you can get full views to the west of the Page Valley, the town of Luray, Massanutten Mountain, Stony Man, Hawksbill, and Marys Rock. Below the platform is a hang-glider launch site.

Many folks stay at Skyland during their visit to the park, and this hike is not only pretty and a good leg stretcher, but it's convenient as well.

Miles and Directions

0.2 Summit of Bushytop. View of Kettle Canyon Skytop to the right. Begin descent on the Millers Head Trail.

0.5 Cement post. Head downhill to observation platform.

0.8 Observation platform on Millers Head. Retrace your steps.

1.6 Back at trailhead.

23 Limberlost

A short walk along a crushed greenstone surface (suitable for wheelchairs) that passes a stand of hemlocks over 400 years old. This trail is ADA accessible.

Skyline Mile: 43.0
Distance: 1.3 miles, loop.
Difficulty: Easy.
Traffic: Moderate to heavy, depending on time of year.

Maps: National Geographic Trails Illustrated Topographic Map 228; Map 10, Appalachian Trail and Other Trails in Shenandoah National Park, Central District (PATC, Inc.).

Finding the trailhead: The trail begins at Mile 43.0 on Skyline Drive. Turn east off the drive at the Limberlost Trail sign. Park at the upper Old Rag Fire Road in a paved lot. Pets are not allowed on this trail.

The Hike

The Limberlost Trail has been designed to be ADA accessible and is the only such trail in the park. However, the path is certainly not limited to that use. The nearly level path is lined with mountain laurel. Until recently, it was also rimmed by ancient hemlock trees, some said to be 400 years old. Sadly, the exotic insect pest known as the wooly adelgid, which sucks the stored food from the hemlock needles, wreaked havoc on Limberlost's hemlocks. Now all are gone, dead, having either fallen or been cut down for safety. The trees will lie in place, gradually decaying into the soil. A different plant life-form will begin to arise now that the sun can reach the forest floor.

The oak trees in Limberlost have also suffered greatly due to gypsy moth invasions. However, wildflowers bloom in spring and summer; white pine, birch, and maple trees still flourish in this beautiful place. Limberlost is truly "the story of a changing forest."

The Limberlost Forest also preserves some of the park's oldest and largest red spruce trees. This species is a remnant from the last ice age, and one such tree is believed to be more than 250 years old. This patriarch stands alone by a small stream that you will encounter along the walk.

Addie Pollock laid the groundwork for preserving the Limberlost

Intervals: Vertical, 50 ft; Horizontal, .5 mi.

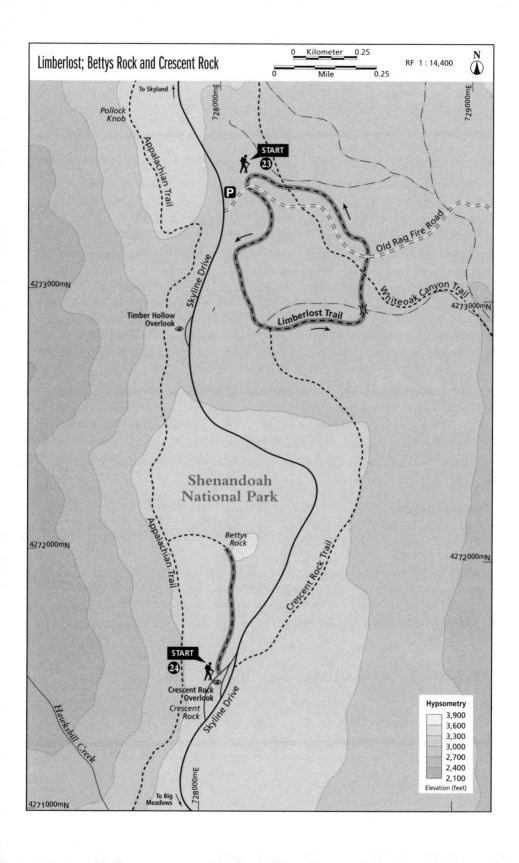

Limberlost; Bettys Rock and Crescent Rock

0   Kilometer   0.25

0   Mile   0.25

RF 1 : 14,400

N

To Skyland

Pollock Knob

Appalachian Trail

728000mE

729000mE

START
23

P

Old Rag Fire Road

Whiteoak Canyon Trail

4273000mN

4273000mN

Timber Hollow Overlook

Limberlost Trail

Skyline Drive

Shenandoah National Park

Appalachian Trail

Crescent Rock Trail

Bettys Rock

4272000mN

4272000mN

START
24

Crescent Rock Overlook

Crescent Rock

Skyline Drive

Hawksbill Creek

728000mE

To Big Meadows

4271000mN

Hypsometry

3,900
3,600
3,300
3,000
2,700
2,400
2,100
Elevation (feet)

Forest. In 1920 she bought one hundred of the largest trees in the area for $1,000. Her husband, George, who established Skyland, named the remnant forest after the Gene Stratton Porter novel *Girl of the Limberlost,* though in that case "limberlost" referred to a fictitious setting in North Carolina.

Because this has been designated an "Outstanding Natural Area," no bicycles, pets, or camping are allowed along the trail in the Limberlost. The newly reconstructed trail was officially dedicated in the summer of 1997.

After parking, read the information on the kiosk and the cement post. Note that other trails radiate from and cross the hardpacked crushed greenstone Limberlost Trail. We chose to hike the path counterclockwise for the following description.

As you meander through what was once an old meadow, notice the abundance of wood benches for resting and observing. There is a bench about every 400 feet. Soon you cross a boardwalk over a wet, swampy area. After 0.4 mile, you encounter a cement post indicating that at this point the Crescent Rock Trail enters the Limberlost Trail from Skyline Drive. The Limberlost Trail proceeds straight ahead and offers yet another lesson in the devastating power of nature. In the fall of 1996, Tropical Storm Fran swept through the area, uprooting many mature trees and causing extensive trail erosion. The latter was repaired in 1997 after several months of work. More recent storms have also caused damage.

At 0.7 mile you cross a large wooden bridge. A sign reads, THIS BRIDGE WAS BUILT IN PARTNERSHIP WITH THE BELL ATLANTIC PIONEERS VIRGINIA OLD DOMINION CHAPTER 43. Beyond that, a cement post points the way to the Whiteoak Canyon Trail access.

Near the trail's end, another cement post shows the Whiteoak Canyon Trail going left and right. Stay on the crushed greenstone trail with the Limberlost markers to the trail's end.

Miles and Directions

0.4 Cement post showing the Crescent Rock Trail going south. Stay on the wooden boardwalk of the Limberlost Trail.

0.7 Cross wooden bridge.

1.0 Cross other trails such as the Whiteoak Canyon Trail, Old Rag Fire Road, Whiteoak Canyon Trail (a second time), and Skyland-Big Meadows Horse Trail. Stay on the Limberlost Trail.

1.3 Trailhead. Loop completed. Back at parking lot.

24 Bettys Rock and Crescent Rock

Two very short hikes with great views.

See map on page 85.
Skyline Mile: 44.4

Distance: Bettys Rock, 550 yards; Crescent Rock, 100 yards.

Difficulty: Easy.

Traffic: Moderate to heavy.

Maps: National Geographic Trails Illustrated Topographic Map 228; Map 10, Appalachian Trail and Other Trails in Shenandoah National Park, Central District (PATC, Inc.).

Finding the trailhead: See map on page 85. The trail begins at Mile 44.4 on Skyline Drive, at the Crescent Rock Overlook. Drive into the overlook to the interpretive sign in the center. Bettys Rock is to your right, 600 yards from the sign; Crescent Rock is on your left.

The Hikes

Both of these short, enjoyable jaunts offer spectacular views to the west of the surrounding mountains and the Shenandoah Valley. Both also offer a brief chance to stretch your legs after following long lines of traffic. On wet days, the rocks on the overlooks can be slick, so watch your children and your footing. In places, the rocks drop off suddenly. No climbing! On the way up to Bettys Rock, witch hazel, oak, and maple trees line the trail. If you hike in the early morning or late afternoon, you'll probably see many deer. From the overlook, you see Hawksbill Mountain to the immediate left. Naked Top is not far from Hawksbill. The Massanutten Range towers across the Shenandoah Valley. You get much the same view from Crescent Rock. However, the hike is 450 yards shorter.

Intervals: Vertical, 50 ft; Horizontal, .1 mi.

25 Cedar Run–Whiteoak Canyon Loop

A very strenuous loop hike through two gorges that passes nine beautiful waterfalls in Cedar Run and Whiteoak Canyon.

Skyline Mile: 45.6

Distance: 8.8 miles, loop.

Difficulty: Strenuous.

Traffic: Light on Cedar Run, heavy in Whiteoak Canyon, especially on weekends.

Maps: National Geographic Trails Illustrated Topographic Map 228; Map 10, Appalachian Trail and Other Trails in Shenandoah National Park, Central District (PATC, Inc.).

Finding the trailhead: The hike begins at Mile 45.6 on Skyline Drive at the Hawksbill Gap parking area. Park on the east side of the road if you can—the trail begins at the cement post. There is additional parking on the west side.

Intervals: Vertical, 500 ft; Horizontal, 1 mi.

The Hike

According to signs on the trailhead, the 6.3-mile descent and return ascent along the Whiteoak Canyon Trail can be made in six hours. That is certainly true, particularly for someone in good shape. However, because the trail takes you to an area of such great natural beauty, it would be far better, and probably necessary, to plan to make this a full-day hike. Pack a picnic lunch, swimsuit, and camera, for the trail puts you within easy access of two beautiful waterfalls, relatively easy access of four more, and not-so-easy access of three others for a total of nine falls.

For this incredibly beautiful yet strenuous hike, you need lots of endurance. The trail takes you straight down an extremely rocky, rough path; it winds through the wilderness and leads through areas of great beauty. Because of the area's precipitous nature, this is one of the few places in the park that was never inhabited. Be sure to carry plenty of water.

The first trail, Cedar Run, is also a place where accidents could easily happen. We both fell on slick rocks. A note, too, about trail maintenance: It is as well cleared as possible and could not be much better given the nature of the terrain. Hike the entire loop only if you have at least six hours. On the descents, it seems each step must be planned; the ascents are steep enough to force a slow pace. However, if you're up to it, the rewards from this hike are among the park's best.

Begin the hike on the Cedar Run Trail at the cement post on the east side of Skyline Drive at the Hawksbill Gap parking area (Mile 45.6). Remain on the Cedar Run Trail and avoid turning onto two other trails that diverge from this trail within the first 100 feet. Simply follow the cement posts that indicate you're on the Cedar Run Trail.

A steep descent begins immediately on this rough, rocky trail that passes through the woods and courses beneath a canopy of oak trees. Soon a dry streambed can be seen to the right, and it isn't long before the flow begins, gently coursing over rocks and into small pools. The peace, beauty, and solitude of

◀ *Cedar Run.*

Cedar Run are a delight. We saw a black bear cub scamper across the trail and into the woods here. Hiking at a slow pace is a necessity since slick rocks of varying sizes are potentially dangerous and demand calculated steps. By going slowly you'll have better glimpses of the surroundings.

At about 1.1 miles you encounter the first view of the lovely falls and pools. For the next 0.6 mile, the beautiful vista continues with a series of falls and pools, giving an understanding to the word "run." It's easy as well to comprehend why this is one of the few areas of the park that was never inhabited or farmed by the mountain folk.

At 1.5 miles the trail crosses Cedar Run on rocks and climbs the opposite bank. Soon it winds back to parallel the stream again. Then the water courses down a steep descent and settles into a gorgeous pool at the base of Half Mile Cliffs. Take time out to soak your feet or dunk yourself. There are no rock faces to climb here, and a more idyllic setting is hard to imagine.

The rocky trail continues, now high above the stream, but still with steep declines. It finally drops to meet the stream at 2.6 miles. Look across the stream to locate the blue blazes on the other side, for this is the crossing point. If you walk as far as the orange blazes on rocks and trees, you'll be on private property. The stream crossing is easy, but beware of the slick rocks.

At 2.8 miles you encounter a cement post. Stay to the left. In order to access the Whiteoak Canyon Trail, which is 0.8 mile farther, the trail splits and becomes the Cedar Run Link Trail. For this next 0.8 mile, the path becomes a delight to sore feet and ankles. No more rocks, just a nice, wide, soft path with gentle ups and downs. The spur leads to a stream crossing (now Whiteoak Run) at about mile 3.6. As you cross, you see a cement post directly in front of you. Take the left trail, which is the Whiteoak Canyon Trail. Skyline Drive is 4.8 miles ahead.

The trail now ascends Whiteoak Canyon. The ascent is quite steep with lots of rocks to scramble around. Great views of waterfalls and pools begin soon. These are closer to the trail than those along the Cedar Run Trail, and they make great picnic and resting spots. They also provide great photographic opportunities, particularly on overcast days. Ideally, you should use a tripod.

After following this path straight up for about 2.5 miles, you encounter a cement post. This is the last waterfall along the route outlined here—and obviously the first for those proceeding from the top. Our route swings right, still climbing. About 0.2 mile later, walk out on the rocks to the left for an awesome view of the falls and the pool below. A nearby sign indicates that camping is prohibited from this point back down to the junction with the spur trail since the area is designated as an "Outstanding Natural Area."

Several trails converge after the viewpoint. Stay left, then right, following the blue blazes uphill to the footbridge on the left. Cross the bridge to the cement post and go left onto the connector path, which parallels the stream for a short distance. The trail swings right onto a wide old road and horse trail—the Whiteoak Fire

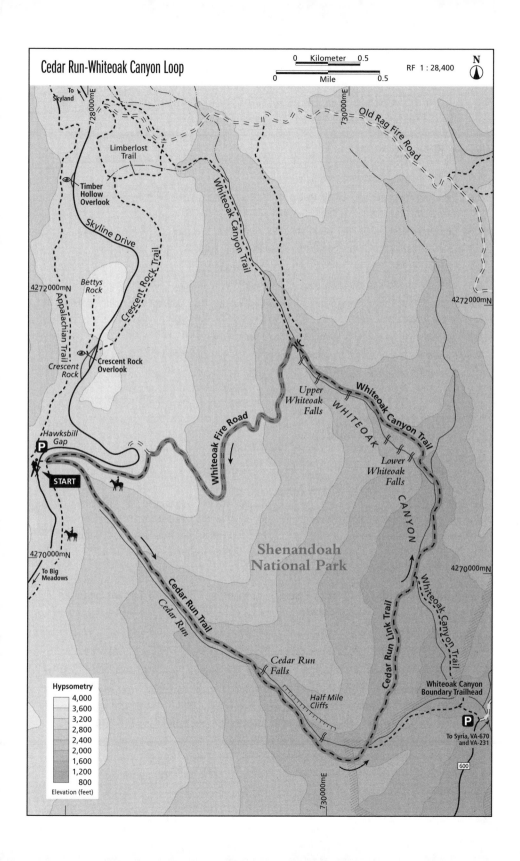

Cedar Run-Whiteoak Canyon Loop

Kilometer 0 0.5

Mile 0 0.5

RF 1 : 28,400

N

To Skyland

728000mE

Old Rag Fire Road

730000mE

Limberlost Trail

Whiteoak Canyon Trail

Timber Hollow Overlook

Skyline Drive

Crescent Rock Trail

4272000mN

Bettys Rock

4272000mN

Appalachian Trail

Crescent Rock Overlook

Crescent Rock

Whiteoak Fire Road

Upper Whiteoak Falls

Whiteoak Canyon Trail

WHITEOAK

Hawksbill Gap

P

START

Lower Whiteoak Falls

CANYON

4270000mN

Shenandoah National Park

4270000mN

To Big Meadows

Cedar Run Trail

Cedar Run

Cedar Run Link Trail

Whiteoak Canyon Trail

Hypsometry

| |
| 4,000 |
| 3,600 |
| 3,200 |
| 2,800 |
| 2,400 |
| 2,000 |
| 1,600 |
| 1,200 |
| 800 |

Elevation (feet)

Cedar Run Falls

Half Mile Cliffs

Whiteoak Canyon Boundary Trailhead

P

To Syria, VA-670 and VA-231

730300mE

600

Road—at about mile 6.6. The ascent is steady and gradual. Finally, at mile 8.3 you encounter a cement post. Turn left and walk a long 0.5 mile on a yellow-blazed horse trail. At the very last cement post, within sight of the road, swing right to the trailhead to complete the loop and return to your vehicle.

Miles and Directions

1.5 Cross Cedar Run and climb the bank.

2.6 Second stream crossing on left. Watch for and follow blue blazes. Do not continue straight on the old road as it enters private property.

2.8 Cement post at split in trail. Go left onto the Cedar Run Link Trail.

3.6 Cross Whiteoak Run to the cement post. Go left, now on the Whiteoak Canyon Trail.

6.1 Cement post at base of first falls. Trail swings to the right.

6.3 Walk out on rocks to the left for beautiful views of falls and pool.

6.6 Cement post. Trail becomes Whiteoak Fire Road. Go left, then right, following blue blazes to the footbridge.

8.3 Cement post. Turn left. It's a long 0.5 mile to your vehicle.

8.8 At last, the trail bears right at another cement post and continues to the trailhead, completing the loop at Hawksbill Gap.

26 Hawksbill Summit

A loop hike to the summit of the park's highest mountain with spectacular views.

Skyline Mile: 45.6
Distance: Either 1.9 miles out and back or 2.8 miles, loop.
Difficulty: Moderate.
Traffic: Moderate to heavy.

Maps: National Geographic Trails Illustrated Topographic Map 228; Map 10, Appalachian Trail and Other Trails in Shenandoah National Park, Central District (PATC, Inc.).

Finding the trailhead: Park at the Hawksbill Gap parking area at Mile 45.6 on Skyline Drive. The trailhead is at the north end of the lot.

The Hike

At 4,051 feet, Hawksbill is the park's highest peak. It's also a good place to see birds. In fact, much of Virginia's endangered peregrine falcon history has been recorded at Hawksbill and several other surrounding park mountains. Since 1989, biologists have raised and released thirty-seven young falcons from Hawksbill and Franklin Cliffs.

Whiteoak Canyon.

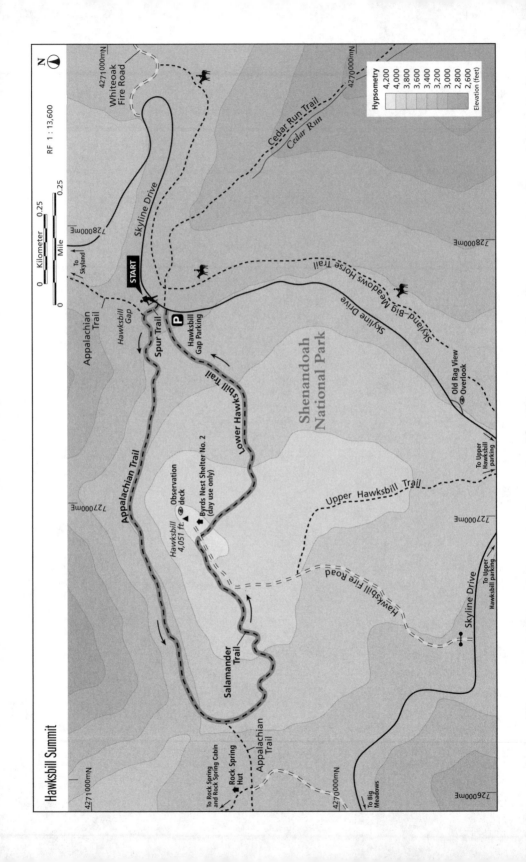

Hawksbill Summit

RF 1 : 13,600

N

In July of 1994, 1996, and 1997, biologists confirmed a pair of peregrines had successfully nested in the park. With luck, you may see peregrines from atop Hawksbill.

Intervals: Vertical, 200 ft; Horizontal, 1 mi.

Several trails lead to the peak, and because the view from the peak is so commanding, the somewhat steep climb is well worth the effort even if you don't see peregrines. Because the loop hike to the summit travels partly along the Appalachian Trail, the trek has added allure. Near the summit the trail passes through an area designated as an "Outstanding Natural Area," which is precisely what the name implies. All along the way, mountain laurel flanks either side of the trail, adding blends of incredible color.

Byrds Nest Shelter No. 2 is located at the summit of Hawksbill. The three-sided structure was built with funds provided by Sen. Harry F. Byrd Sr. and is one of four such shelters in the park. No water is available at the site, and camping is not permitted on or near the summit.

The trail begins at the north end of the Hawksbill Gap parking lot at Mile 45.6 on Skyline Drive. A level spur trail about 100 yards long leads to the Appalachian Trail, which is marked with white slashes. Turn south (left) onto the AT and begin climbing. The trail is rocky and, as always, good hiking boots are recommended. Within 0.4 mile the trail approaches a rock slide. After another 25 yards, it passes a second talus slope, and you will have a view of mountains and valleys spilling off to the west. Half a mile from the trailhead, the trail approaches a rock-strewn outcropping, suggestive once again of the erosion of the park's mountains. Lichens cover the rocks, and here and there trees struggle for a foothold in soils formed relatively recently.

Toward the summit, foxtail blooms in great abundance. Columbine also rears its head, as does a species of geranium. Several rock outcrops tilt upward, revealing layers that look like a stack of pancakes. The area is one of outstanding natural splendor.

About a mile along the trail, you come to a cement post noting the mileage along the AT and the distance to the Rock Spring Cabin. The post points toward Hawksbill and back toward Fishers Gap. Make a hard left onto the Salamander Trail at this point and continue climbing. The summit is only 0.9 mile away. Within 0.25 mile of the junction, the rocks covering the trail become more exposed, probably the result of tremendous spring runoff. Near the top, the trail joins a fire road. Keep climbing to the summit, not far away. There, you find Byrds Nest Shelter No. 2. No water is available at the site, and camping is not permitted on or near the summit.

The shelter is surrounded by red spruce, balsam fir, and mountain ash. Continue the last few yards to the observation platform, and you are standing on the highest point in the park.

The view from the top of Hawksbill is commanding and panoramic. Mountains roll off in all directions, blending gradually into yet more mountains in the hazy distance. Within the cement overlook, the Park Service has placed a huge compass, which helps those with maps to orient themselves. Stony Man with its jagged features is to the north, while Brown Mountain spreads neatly to the east. To the south is Graves Mountain. Just below, Skyline Drive threads through the hardwood forest. The town of Luray lies to the northwest.

To return to Hawksbill Gap from the summit, retrace your steps to the shelter and take the fire road to its left (south). This leads very shortly to a cement post. Turn left onto the Lower Hawksbill Trail and follow it for 0.7 mile to the parking lot. The descent is steep and the going a bit slow for some.

Although it seems that returning to Hawksbill Gap involves fairly easy route finding, the series of trails that ascend—and descend—can be confusing. Make sure you follow the metal bands on the cement posts that take you back to Hawksbill Gap or you'll have to hike an additional mile along Skyline Drive.

To make the shorter out-and-back hike of 1.9 miles, access the Lower Hawksbill Trail near the center of the parking lot at Hawksbill Gap. The trail begins in the woods and ascends steeply for about 0.7 mile to a cement post near the summit. Turn right and go another 0.1 mile, passing Byrds Nest Shelter No.2 and reaching the observation deck at the summit. Retrace your steps.

Miles and Directions

0.5 First of three talus slopes, some views.

1.0 Cement post. Make hard left onto the Salamander Trail.

1.9 Hawksbill Summit and observation deck.

2.1 Cement post below and left of the shelter. Turn left onto the Lower Hawksbill Trail.

2.8 Parking lot at Hawksbill Gap. End of loop hike.

27 Rose River

The trail provides access to a number of pools and cascades, including Rose River Falls.

Skyline Mile: 49.4
Distance: 4 miles, loop.
Difficulty: Moderate.
Traffic: Moderate.

Maps: National Geographic Trails Illustrated Topographic Map 228; Map 10, Appalachian Trail and Other Trails in Shenandoah National Park, Central District (PATC, Inc.).

Finding the trailhead: Park at Mile 49.4 at the Fishers Gap Overlook parking lot on the west side of Skyline Drive. Walk to the north end and cross the drive to the east. Go down the fire

road to a cement post. Turn left onto the Rose River Loop Trail (blazed yellow at first, then veer right later at the blue blaze).

The Hike

Rose River Falls is a delightful series of large cascades that drop gently over a distance of several hundred yards. After each rush, the creek and its falls seem to regroup at a quiet pool, then hurry forward once again. You can follow the trail down to the falls and retrace your steps, but it is much more rewarding to make this a loop hike, dropping down to the falls, then continuing out and back along the Hogcamp Branch, eventually returning to the Fishers Gap Overlook parking lot via the wide and heavily-used Rose River Fire Road.

Begin by descending on the Rose River Fire Road. Within 100 feet you see a cement post with the familiar aluminum strip noting the distances. From the post to Rose River Falls, it's 1.2 miles—as the sign notes. Turn left onto the yellow-blazed Skyland-Big Meadows Horse Trail and follow it for 0.6 mile to another cement post. The horse trail goes left (north). Stay right on the blue-blazed Rose River Loop Trail.

Within another 0.5 mile the trail approaches the Rose River and begins to parallel it. The Rose River is immediately attractive. It presents itself as a delightful stream of short cascades, natural flutes and small pools, and steep but abbreviated banks. The trail veers away from the falls, then quickly returns to parallel the creek. Again, it presents itself as a series of small pools and brief drops.

All too soon the trail leaves the Rose River and assumes a more southerly course. At 1.9 miles from the trailhead, a cement block lies mysteriously in the trail. Rooted in the cement are metal rods with nuts. Perhaps it had something to do with the old copper mine site, uphill on the right. At 2.1 miles from the trailhead, the trail approaches the Hogcamp Branch and, in about 100 feet, crosses the creek on a bridge. The trail climbs, still paralleling Hogcamp Branch, which also contains its share of pools and runs. At 2.9 miles the trail links with the lower Dark Hollow Falls Trail and to the Dark Hollow parking lot; the falls are only a short climb away (0.3 mile). The trail crosses the nearby bridge, which also provides access to the trail up Dark Hollow Falls. On the north side of the bridge—the north side of Hogcamp

Intervals: Vertical, 200 ft; Horizontal, 1 mi.

Branch—you'll encounter another cement post directing you to turn right (north) onto the Rose River Fire Road leading to the parking area at the Fishers Gap Overlook, thus completing the loop hike.

Miles and Directions

0.6 Cement post. Stay straight on the blue-blazed trail. The Skyland-Big Meadows Horse Trail heads off to the left (north).

1.0 Trail turns sharply to the right.

1.2 Top of Rose River Falls.

1.7 Trail bears right, ascending Hogcamp Branch.

1.8 Old copper mine on right.

1.9 Cross Hogcamp Branch on bridge, staying on trail. Do not turn left.

2.9 Cement post and junction with the Rose River Fire Road. Turn right, cross Hogcamp Branch, stay to right on the fire road (or turn left for a 0.6 mile out-and-back trip to Dark Hollow Falls).

4.0 Cross Skyline Drive, return to the Fishers Gap Overlook parking area, ending the loop hike.

28 Dark Hollow Falls

A short out-and-back hike to one of the park's most popular and easily accessible falls.

Skyline Mile: 50.7
Distance: 1.4 miles out and back.
Difficulty: Moderately strenuous in, strenuous out.
Traffic: Heavy, highest use in the park.

Maps: National Geographic Trails Illustrated Topographic Map 228; Map 10, Appalachian Trail and Other Trails in Shenandoah National Park, Central District (PATC, Inc.).

Finding the trailhead: The trail begins at Mile 50.7 on Skyline Drive.

The Hike

The trail descends from the parking lot and follows Hogcamp Branch. At 0.6 mile you encounter an overlook of 70-foot Dark Hollow Falls. Along the trail, you encounter rails that shouldn't require a statement of intent but apparently do, because invariably some fail to realize that not only are the fences intended to prevent further erosion but also to save life and limb. This is one place with a history of injury. Please remain on the trail! Rocks can be wet and very slippery. Pets are not allowed on this trail.

Continue for another 0.1 mile to the base of Dark Hollow Falls. If you enjoy the spectacle, be aware that you're in good company. According to a resident naturalist,

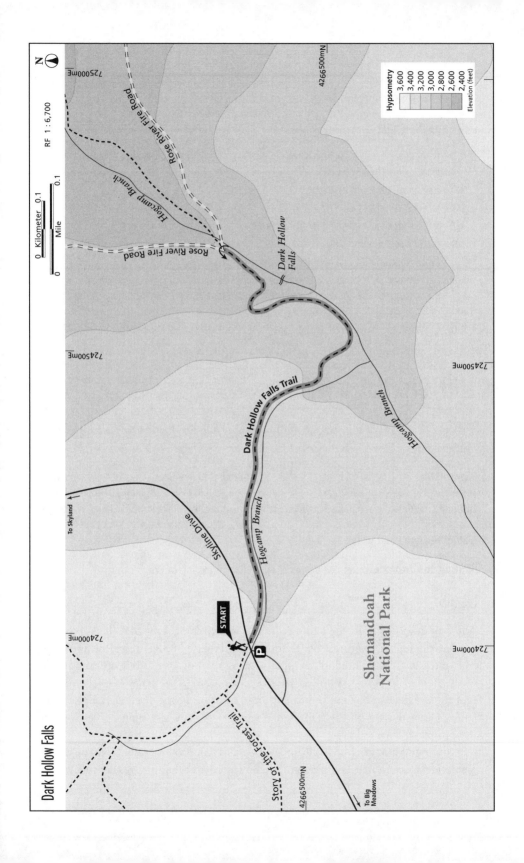

this scene was once appreciated by Thomas Jefferson.

Intervals: Vertical, 200 ft; Horizontal, .2 mi.

The falls are obviously appealing, especially if you consider their source. Hogcamp Branch drains the Big Meadow Swamp, which can be relatively dry during some of the summer. Nevertheless, Hogcamp manages to gather enough water in its progression toward Dark Hollow Falls to create a lovely falls. You can descend farther to enjoy yet other falls created by Hogcamp Branch, or you can return to the trailhead. From the base of Dark Hollow Falls, you will climb 0.7 mile and about 440 feet in elevation to your starting point.

The descent to the falls is the easy part of the hike. A few benches have been placed along the trail to provide you with opportunities to rest on the return trip and to reflect on the area's scenic beauty.

Miles and Directions

0.6 Overlook of Dark Hollow Falls.

0.7 Base of Dark Hollow Falls

1.4 Return to starting point.

29 Story of the Forest Trail

An easy, one- to two-hour, interpretive, round-trip hike on a trail showing plant succession in the surrounding Blue Ridge forest.

Skyline Mile: 51.0
Distance: 1.8 miles, loop.
Difficulty: Easy.
Traffic: Moderate to heavy.

Maps: National Geographic Trails Illustrated Topographic Map 228; Map 10, Appalachian Trail and Other Trails in Shenandoah National Park, Central District (PATC, Inc.).

Finding the trailhead: The trail begins at Mile 51.0, across Skyline Drive from the Harry F. Byrd Sr. Visitor Center. Stay on the paved path to the right.

The Hike

This delightful, informative walk is a self-guided tour to the wonders of a Blue Ridge forest. This is a hike for everyone, especially children, as they'll probably get good views of wildlife. Pets are not allowed on the trail.

At the trailhead, bear right (the maintenance area is to the left). You are on a wide trail, suitable for all ages. The trail is gravel, then forest floor, then paved.

The first part of this hike is 0.8 mile long and well marked. After that section, turn left and head south via the paved biking/walking path back to the visitor center, adding another mile to your route.

Miles and Directions

0.2 Bridge over Hogcamp Branch. Reach a junction shortly, stay left.

0.4 Junction with horse trail. Proceed straight.

Intervals: Vertical, 25 ft; Horizontal, .5 mi.

0.8 Proceed straight to the Big Meadows Campground. Turn left to access the paved path back to the visitor center.

1.8 Return to the starting point on the bike trail.

30 Big Meadows

Follow paths through a landscape probably created by Native Americans and maintained as such because of long use by the mountain people and by the Park Service.

See map on page 102.
Skyline Mile: 51.0
Distance: Walk the maze of trails until you tire.
Difficulty: Easy.
Traffic: Heavy.

Maps: National Geographic Trails Illustrated Topographic Map 228; Map 10, Appalachian Trail and Other Trails in Shenandoah National Park, Central District (PATC, Inc.).

Finding the trailhead: The trail begins at Mile 51.0, across Skyline Drive from the Harry F. Byrd Sr. Visitor Center at Big Meadows.

The Hike

As you hike, remember that Big Meadows has a known geologic history of close to 40,000 years, during which time the climate varied from tropical to that of northern Canada. Archaeologists know that American Indians first hunted and camped in the meadow nearly 8,000 years ago when the climate was colder. These early hunters may have used fire to keep the area open, but there is no scientific evidence to verify this.

In the late eighteenth century, homesteaders moved into the area and took advantage of the clearing the Native Americans had created to farm and graze their livestock. Today, just beyond the meadow, you can still find the foundations and root cellars of these mountain people's homes.

Subsequent to the park's establishment, Big Meadows has served many purposes. In 1933 it became the setting for a large Civilian Conservation Corps camp. On July 3, 1936, the meadow was the site of the park's dedication, with President Franklin D. Roosevelt presiding. During World War II, over 2,000 soldiers with the Army Corps of Engineers camped in the meadow.

To thwart intrusions from the surrounding forest and maintain the meadow in its historical condition, park rangers have used a variety of techniques, including mowing, spraying, and controlled burning.

The meadow offers sanctuary for a variety of wildlife, including deer, some of which are quite tame. If they approach you, please don't feed them because the micro flora in their stomachs can't process human food. Hand feeding also decreases their fear of humans, and thus their chance of survival during hunting season should they wander out of the park.

So don't feed the deer!

There is no official trail through Big Meadows, though there is a series of trails, some of which have been created by decades of use by game animals. Others, of course, have been enhanced by people. All paths are quite easy to see and wander. Ranger-led tours depart frequently from the visitor center.

One trail does course throughout the meadow and, because of continuous use, is better defined than most of the others. This path begins at the parking area east of Skyline Drive, directly across from the filling station at the turnoff into Big Meadows. The trail is on the left, just beyond the chain that crosses the Rapidan Fire Road. You are pretty much on your own here; the distance across the meadow is less than a mile, and you can wander at will.

You're likely to find an abundance of wildlife in the meadow, including deer. Study the different types of grasses. Look at the herbs and the incredible variety of wildflowers. See the milkweed and asters? Notice the blueberries and the shrub with the dogwoodlike leaves; it is the panicled dogwood, which is rare and in need of protection.

As you continue your walk, look for the various species of trees, such as the black locust, that grow along the edge of the meadow. Edges are important to wildlife because they provide a transition from areas that offer food to areas that offer protection. Park managers have used fire to prevent the encroachment of black locust and maintain these edges. Shenandoah is fortunate to have such a prairielike habitat. This is the only sustained meadow in the park, and it currently encompasses about 134 acres.

When you tire, simply wander back to your vehicle. If you're lucky, you'll be more keenly aware of the rich biological diversity that is inherent in Shenandoah National Park.

31 Lewis Spring Falls Trail

A loop trail through the hardwood forest, descending to 81-foot Lewis Spring Falls and climbing out again.

See map on page 102.
Skyline Mile: 51.2
Distance: 3.3 miles, loop.
Difficulty: Moderate.
Traffic: Light to moderate.

Maps: National Geographic Trails Illustrated Topographic Map 228; Map 10, Appalachian Trail and Other Trails in Shenandoah National Park, Central District (PATC, Inc.).

A view from an overlook at Lewis Spring Falls. ▶

Finding the trailhead: Exit Skyline Drive at Mile 51.2 at the Big Meadows complex. Leave from the amphitheater across the road from the Big Meadows Campground, 0.7 mile from the visitor center.

The Hike

At 81 feet in height, Lewis Spring Falls is the fourth-highest falls in the park. It's a beautiful, gentle falls, cascading from two creeks and then descending to a false bottom where it spills once again. The falls often branches, depending on the time of year. You have a commanding view of the falls from an overlook constructed by young men working in Civilian Conservation Corps camps in the 1930s, which offers a safe and contained view.

Access the amphitheater behind the picnic area. Below the amphitheater, at the cement post, pick up the blue blazes of the Lewis Spring Falls Trail, which branches to the right off the Appalacian Trail. (If you were to stay on the AT, Milam Gap is 2.6 miles south, Fishers Gap is 1.6 miles north.)

This well-maintained trail descends immediately and continues to do so for about 1 mile. The rocky trail requires sturdy hiking boots. Watch yourself on the rocks—even dry ones can be slippery. Notice the many fallen trees, evidence of the power of ice and wind storms.

The path is flanked on both sides by hardwood trees and low-growth bushes. You will descend into a hollow with some granite outcroppings. Stay alert for wildlife. Deer abound, and on our hike we ran into one of the forest's spotted skunks. Though the animal lifted its tail, it also lowered it as we backed off, so we carried no bad smell back to our tent.

When the trail finally levels, you can hear the falls, then another brief ascent brings you to a nice overlook with views to the western mountains. Turn left, to the southeast, and follow the blue blazes to the observation point. You cross a small stream and parallel an iron railing. Don't attempt to climb down to the falls. People have suffered serious, even fatal, falls trying this.

From the overlook, backtrack north for about 50 feet and pick up the blue blazes going east. The trail maintains an uphill grade, sure and steady. It parallels a creek on your right and then switchbacks away from the stream.

After climbing for 0.6 mile, you reach a cement marker. Go east for 70 yards on the Lewis Spring Fire Road, then turn north (left) onto the AT. Follow the white blazes on the trees. From this point (you're still chugging uphill), the Big Meadows Lodge is another 1.4 miles. The campground is 0.5 mile beyond that.

Intervals: Vertical, 200 ft; Horizontal, 1 mi.

Be sure to carry water on this hike. There are several signs cautioning you not to drink the water along the way. Some is CONTAMINATED, say the signs, and requires VIGOROUS BOILING. One common contaminant is *Giardia*, a waterborne parasite that can cause severe diarrhea, cramps, and fatigue. The parasite can survive in very cold water and is spread by the droppings of dogs, horses, cattle, elk, rabbits, and other small mammals, as well as humans.

Alternative hike 31a: For families with children under the age of nine or ten, the hike described above to Lewis Spring Falls may be too strenuous. A somewhat shorter, easier alternative descends a wide, gravel service road that is just south of the Big Meadows complex. This hike is 2.5 miles round-trip and has an elevation gain and loss of about 800 feet. If you're hiking with young children, it may take longer. Be sure to carry sufficient water. You pass yellow-blazed horse trails to the left and right and come to a junction with the Appalachian Trail at 0.3 mile. Just past the junction, take the blue-blazed Lewis Falls Trail on your left. Follow that for 0.6 mile to another junction. Take the spur trail to your left, which leads to a nice overlook near the top of the falls. Retrace your steps from this point, going mostly uphill.

Miles and Directions

0.1   Amphitheater and junction with AT. Take the Lewis Spring Falls Trail behind the amphitheater (blue blazes) and begin descent.

1.0   View to west. Turn south to overlook.

1.3   Observation point of falls 250 feet ahead. Backtrack to main trail.

1.9   Cement post. Go east 70 yards to access the Appalachian Trail.

3.3   AT back to amphitheater.

32 Blackrock

A very short and easy walk to a rocky viewpoint offering good views.

Skyline Mile: 51.2
Distance: 0.4 mile out and back.
Difficulty: Easy.
Traffic: Moderate to heavy.

Maps: National Geographic Trails Illustrated Topographic Map 228; Map 10, Appalachian Trail and Other Trails in Shenandoah National Park, Central District (PATC, Inc.).

Finding the trailhead: From Skyline Drive, turn north into the Big Meadows complex and proceed 0.9 mile to the dining hall at the Big Meadows Lodge. The trailhead is at the far end of the lodge parking lot beyond the dining hall.

The Hike

The trail is well marked with a sign in the parking lot. Begin a leisurely ascent to the viewpoint (3,721 feet). On clear days, you have excellent views to the left and right. Use caution: The rocks here are quite slick. This is a nice stroll, especially in the evening when town lights below are lit.

Intervals: Vertical, 25 ft; Horizontal, .1 mi.

33 Rapidan Camp–Laurel Prong–Hazeltop Loop

A moderately difficult hike to a falls, to the retreat of a former U.S. president, and a return along one of the park's higher and more geologically interesting peaks.

Skyline Mile: 53.0
Distance: 7.4 miles loop, or 4.2 miles out and back.
Difficulty: Strenuous.
Traffic: Light.

Maps: National Geographic Trails Illustrated Topographic Map 228; Map 10, Appalachian Trail and Other Trails in Shenandoah National Park, Central District (PATC, Inc.).

Finding the trailhead: The trail begins at Milam Gap at Mile 53.0 on Skyline Drive.

The Hike

Of the original thirteen structures that once formed Rapidan Camp, only three remain today: the Brown House (which has been fully restored, inside and out), the Creel Cabin, and the Prime Minister's Cabin. The setting is attractive—and certainly as beautiful today as it was when the former president retreated to Shenandoah. Hoover was searching for three features: (1) His retreat had to be within 100 miles of Washington D.C.; (2) the retreat had to be located on a trout stream; and (3) it had to be at least 2,500 feet above sea level. Because of the camp's significance, the Department of the Interior designated the area a National Historic Landmark in 1988. Rapidan Camp is closed to backcountry camping.

The trail begins from the south side of the Milam Gap parking lot, located just a little north of Mile 53.0. To reach the trailhead walk across Skyline Drive to the side opposite the parking lot and decide whether you wish to make this a loop hike or a 2.1-mile hike down the Mill Prong Trail to Rapidan Camp and back for a total of 4.2 miles. We elected to make this a 7.4-mile loop hike, traveling first to Rapidan Camp and then back along the Laurel Prong Trail, linking with the Appalachian

Brown House.

Trail. Many others along the route reversed the loop.

The trail gradually descends and soon begins to follow Mill Prong. Shortly thereafter a sign explains that this is a catch-and-release creek. The sign reads: ALL FISH MUST BE HANDLED CAREFULLY AND RETURNED IMMEDIATELY TO THE STREAM. ONLY ARTIFICIAL FLIES OR LURES WITH A SINGLE HOOK ARE PERMITTED. At about 1.9 miles, you will pass a junction with the Rapidan Fire Road. Stay straight on the Mill Prong Trail.

The trail continues downhill, quickly reaching Rapidan Camp, for a total of 2.1 miles. Once you reach the camp, explore the surroundings. In addition to the various structures, two streams converge near the camp—Laurel Prong and Mill Prong—both of which combine to create the Rapidan River. The river is full of deep pools that still contain the trout that enticed President Hoover. Retrace your steps here for 4.2 miles out and back, or continue.

To make this a loop hike, take the Laurel Prong Trail, which departs near the Rapidan Camp parking lot. Within 100 yards you encounter a maintenance road, which goes uphill to the right. Ignore the spur road and follow the trail marked with a yellow slash.

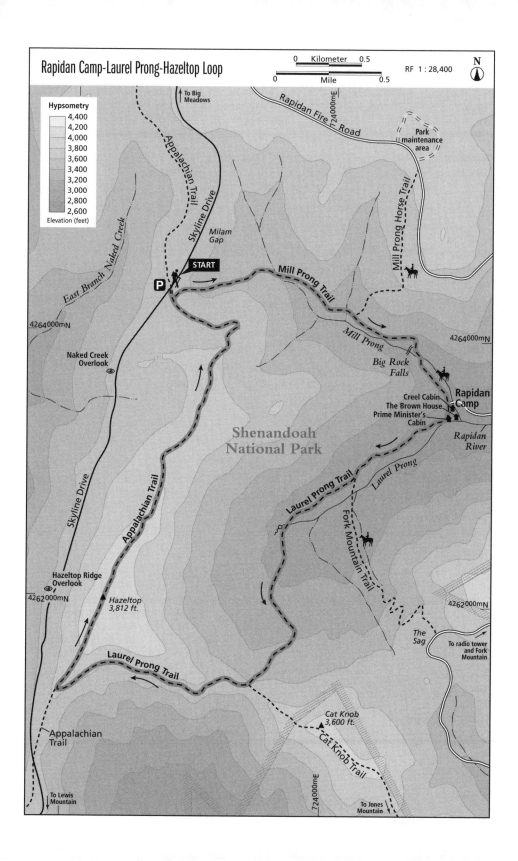

Rapidan Camp-Laurel Prong-Hazeltop Loop

Kilometer
RF 1 : 28,400

0   Mile   0.5

N

Hypsometry

4,400
4,200
4,000
3,800
3,600
3,400
3,200
3,000
2,800
2,600
Elevation (feet)

Appalachian Trail

Skyline Drive

Rapidan Fire Road

Park maintenance area

Mill Prong Horse Trail

To Big Meadows

Milam Gap

START

P

Mill Prong Trail

Mill Prong

Big Rock Falls

4264000mN

4264000mN

East Branch Naked Creek

Naked Creek Overlook

Creel Cabin
The Brown House
Prime Minister's Cabin

Rapidan Camp

Rapidan River

Shenandoah National Park

Appalachian Trail

Skyline Drive

Laurel Prong Trail

Laurel Prong

Fork Mountain Trail

Hazeltop Ridge Overlook

4262000mN

Hazeltop 3,812 ft.

4262000mN

The Sag

To radio tower and Fork Mountain

Laurel Prong Trail

Appalachian Trail

Cat Knob 3,600 ft.

Cat Knob Trail

724000mE

To Lewis Mountain

724000mE

To Jones Mountain

In 0.4 mile the trail meets the Fork Mountain Trail. Take the right fork to stay on the Laurel Prong Trail. Within 0.1 mile the trail will cross four or five (depending on the time of year) streams, after which it continues its gradual ascent. In about 1 mile the trail intersects with a trail marked by a cement post and the typical metal plate. On one side of the post the inscriptions point the way to the Cat Knob Trail and the Jones Mountain Trail, a distance of about 0.5 mile. Take the right fork to the AT, about 1 mile uphill. Just before accessing the AT, the Laurel Prong Trail becomes fairly steep and rocky. When the Laurel Prong Trail meets the AT, your route proceeds in a northerly direction. The climb continues to Hazeltop (3,812 feet) and then begins a thoroughly delightful descent. The trail is wide, well maintained, and generally free of rocks.

Alternative hike 33a: To reach Big Rock Falls, take the Mill Prong Trail for a 3.4-mile out-and-back hike. Though not one of the park's more spectacular falls, Big Rock Falls is deserving of a visit. It cascades down a long slope and then settles into a quiet little pool. The hike is relatively easy and provides a nice family excursion. The trail departs from Milam Gap.

Alternative hike 33b: To hike Milam Gap to Hazeltop (at 3,812 feet, the third-highest point in the park) and back, the Park Service recommends following the last segment of the above loop from Milam Gap for 4.2 miles out and back.

Miles and Directions

1.7 Big Rock Falls.

1.9 Junction with the Rapidan Fire Road.

2.1 Rapidan Camp.

2.5 Junction with the Fork Mountain Trail. Turn right onto the Laurel Prong Trail.

4.8 The Appalachian Trail; turn right (north).

5.3 Hazeltop Mountain.

7.4 Milam Gap, to complete circuit.

Intervals: Vertical, 400 ft; Horizontal, 1 mi.

34 Bearfence Mountain

A short hike with a 360-degree view and a real rock scramble toward the summit.

Skyline Mile: 56.4
Distance: 1.2 miles, lariat.
Difficulty: Moderate.
Traffic: Moderate to heavy.

Maps: National Geographic Trails Illustrated Topographic Map 228; Map 10, Appalachian Trail and Other Trails in Shenandoah National Park, Central District (PATC, Inc.).

Finding the trailhead: Park at the Bearfence Mountain parking lot, Mile 56.4 on the west side of Skyline Drive. Cross the drive to the east side to a cement post and take the Bearfence Mountain Trail going southeast. Follow the blue blazes.

The Hike

Bearfence Mountain (3,640 feet) is one of several summits in the park that commands a complete panoramic view. Once you have reached the top, you are able to see Massanutten Mountain and the Shenandoah Valley to the west and Laurel Gap, Fork Mountain, and Bluff Mountain to the east. In the short hike from the parking lot to the summit, you pass through the sandstone of the Swift Run Formation, capped by Catoctin basalt. Pets are not allowed on this trail.

Hiking to the summit requires some degree of coordination. Though expertise in rock climbing is not necessary, you need some dexterity to maneuver through jumbled rocks. In some cases, you may find yourself scooting along on your bottom. To ensure good traction and to diminish the possibility of bruised feet, we recommend that you wear good hiking boots, although they won't help much if the rocks are wet or covered with snow. In the summer, park officials have seen rattlesnakes in the area, so watch where you place your feet and hands. Park handouts indicate this is not a trail for small children, especially those who must be carried.

The hike to Bearfence begins at Mile 56.4 on the east side of Skyline Drive, across the road from the Bearfence Mountain parking lot. Almost immediately after leaving the parking lot, you begin to climb uphill. In several places, you see trees (felled by the many severe storms since 1996) whose giant, exposed roots provide mute testimony to the humbling power of nature.

Within 300 yards of the parking lot, the trail begins to thread through huge boulders. This rock was originally volcanic lava, but with millions of years of compression it has metamorphosed into the gray-green rock you see before you today. Appropriately, it is called greenstone, but only recent fractures reveal the green coloration.

If you are out of shape, it may seem as if the torturous maze of boulders will never end, but in reality you begin to break into the open within a few hundred yards. You know you've reached the summit when you can peer down on everything. Looking east, you can see mountains ranging from Hazeltop to Kirtley. Looking west, you can

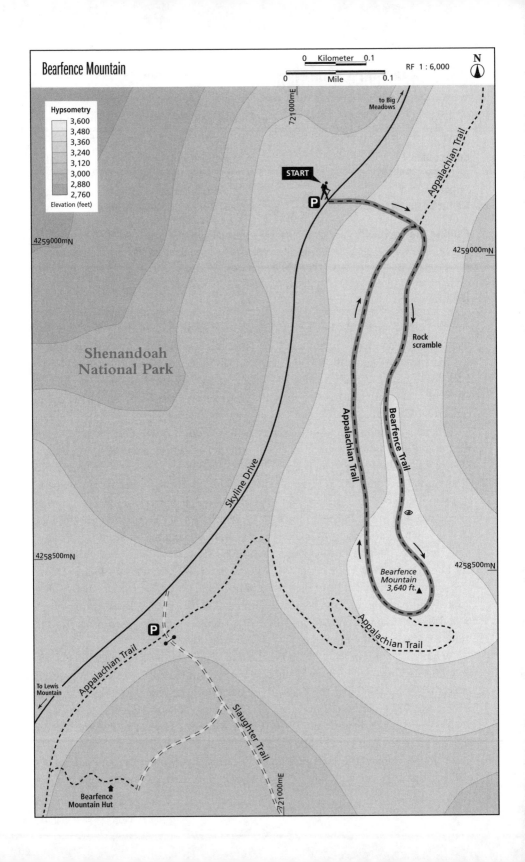

Bearfence Mountain

Hypsometry
- 3,600
- 3,480
- 3,360
- 3,240
- 3,120
- 3,000
- 2,880
- 2,760

Elevation (feet)

N

RF 1 : 6,000

Kilometer 0.1

Mile 0.1

Shenandoah
National Park

START

to Big
Meadows

Appalachian Trail

Rock
scramble

Appalachian Trail

Bearfence Trail

Bearfence
Mountain
3,640 ft.

Appalachian Trail

Skyline Drive

Appalachian Trail

To Lewis
Mountain

Slaughter Trail

Bearfence
Mountain Hut

721000mE

4259000mN

4258500mN

4259000mN

4258500mN

721000mE

see Skyline Drive, the Shenandoah Valley, and Devils Tanyard. You are standing 3,640 feet above sea level, and the view is magnificent.

From Bearfence Mountain, you can retrace your steps to the trailhead for a total hike of 0.8 mile, or you can continue on toward the Appalachian Trail, which you reach very shortly. At the cement post, take the AT north for about 0.7 mile back to the parking lot, for a trek of 1.2 miles.

Miles and Directions

Intervals: Vertical, 50 ft; Horizontal, .4 mi.

200 yards Cross the Appalachian Trail.

0.4 Bearfence Mountain summit.

0.5 AT junction. Turn right and descend.

1.1 Turn left onto the main Bearfence Trail.

1.2 Return to the parking lot.

35 Lewis Mountain Trail

Leading directly from the Lewis Mountain Campground, this hike makes a pleasant short stroll for adults and a small adventure for children.

Skyline Mile: 57.5
Distance: 1 mile out and back.
Difficulty: Easy.
Traffic: Moderate.

Maps: National Geographic Trails Illustrated Topographic Map 228; Map 10, Appalachian Trail and Other Trails in Shenandoah National Park, Central District (PATC, Inc.).

Finding the trailhead: The trail begins at the Lewis Mountain Campground at Mile 57.5 on Skyline Drive, at Campsite 16.

The Hike

If you're not camping at Lewis Mountain, you may park either at the picnic area or at the camp store, then walk the short distance through the campground to Campsite 16, where the trail begins. Follow the blue blazes.

What a great hike this is for imaginative kids! Children can conjure images of trolls and bears as they hike up the path, overgrown on all sides with mosses and ferns.

This hike is not too big on scenery, though, even at the summit, as trees have grown enough to block the views. However, it's a fun stroll that ascends very gently to the top of Lewis Mountain on land once owned by John Lewis, a surveyor for George Washington.

At the summit backtrack to Campsite 16. For a longer trek, you can hike south on the Appalachian Trail to the Pocosin Mission Trail (see Hike 36).

Lewis Mountain Trail

0   Kilometer   0.2

0   Mile   0.2

RF 1 : 12,300

N

Hypsometry
3,600
3,400
3,200
3,000
2,800
2,600
Elevation (feet)

To Big Meadows

Appalachian Trail

P

Skyline Drive

Lewis Mountain Campground

START

Shenandoah National Park

Lewis Mountain 3,570 ft.

Appalachian Trail

To Swift Run Gap

720000mE

4257000mN

720000mE

4257000mN

721000mE

Miles and Directions

0.1   Junction with the Appalachian Trail. Do not access it. Stay left.

0.5   Tree-covered summit. Trail ends. Backtrack from here.

1.0   Campsite 16.

Intervals: Vertical, 50 ft; Horizontal, .25 mi.

36 Pocosin Trail

An inspiring venture along an easy trail providing insights into Shenandoah's history and wildlife.

Skyline Mile: 59.5
Distance: 2.2 miles out and back.
Difficulty: Easy.
Traffic: Light.

Maps: National Geographic Trails Illustrated Topographic Map 228; Map 10, Appalachian Trail and Other Trails in Shenandoah National Park, Central District (PATC, Inc.).

Finding the trailhead: Park about 50 yards down the yellow-blazed Pocosin Fire Road at Mile 59.5 on the east side of Skyline Drive. Pass the chain and follow the fire road.

The Hike

Locate the trailhead by driving first to Mile 59.5 on Skyline Drive. Then turn left onto the Pocosin Fire Road on the east side of the drive. Park near the yellow chain

Ruins at Pocosin Mission.

and begin your hike down the fire road, which proceeds in an easterly direction and crosses the Appalachian Trail in 0.1 mile. In 0.2 mile it approaches the Pocosin Cabin, one in a chain of cabins that serve hikers using the AT. The cabins are managed by the Potomac Appalachian Trail Club (PATC) and are available for rent. To visit the cabin (if unoccupied), turn right onto the side path.

Continue along the fire road, which begins a slight descent. Throughout the spring and summer—and sometimes into the fall—wildflowers flank the trail. Look for columbine in the late spring and for milkweed in the summer. The latter is associated with disturbed sites.

Soon the trail levels, and after about 1 mile you encounter a cement post, indicating the Pocosin Horse Trail (yellow blazes). Turn right onto the Pocosin Horse Trail and look immediately to the left at what seems to be an old mountain cabin. This is actually part of the ruins of an Episcopal mission established around 1904. Near the ruined cabin is all that remains of the old church: its stone steps.

A PATC cabin off of Pocosin Fire Road.

Though the forest is swallowing the artifacts of the period, a number of features from the mission days remain. Old stone stairs and crumbling mission walls are among them. Hiking the several trails that take you to the old mission provides a rewarding excursion, but remember that old timbers and dilapidated rock walls attract snakes, so watch where you're going and where you put your hands. Once you've finished exploring, retrace your steps.

Note: If you're full of energy and wish to explore farther, continue on the Pocosin Horse Trail, cross a stream, and make a gentle ascent. Watch for snakes in this area, as it is often overgrown. About 1.3 miles from the mission site, a marker indicates a right turn on the main trail. Go left for about 0.1 mile to visit the South River Cemetery, still in use. The park boundary is only 0.1 mile away. Retrace your steps to the parking lot for a hike of about 5 miles out and back.

Alternative hike 36a: The Pocosin Mission can also be accessed from the Lewis Mountain Campground at Mile 57.5 on Skyline Drive. Although this route adds another 3.4 miles, it is a delightful trek that follows the Appalachian Trail, and on a cool summer's day the extra distance will hardly be noticed. Access this alternative route from Campsite 16 of the Lewis Mountain Campground. About 70 feet along the trail to Lewis Mountain, you will encounter the Appalachian Trail. Follow the AT south (right) for 1.7 miles to the Pocosin Cabin. Proceed along the Pocosin Fire Road (as described above) to the mission. Return along the same route—back to the AT going north, which will return you to the campground for a total of 5.6 miles out and back.

Miles and Directions

0.1 Cement post. Stay on the fire road as it crosses the Appalachian Trail.

0.2 Cement post. Stay on the fire road. PATC Pocosin Cabin (locked) to right.

1.0 Cement post. Junction with the Pocosin Horse Trail and Pocosin Hollow Trail to the left. Turn right onto the Pocosin Horse Trail and follow the yellow blazes.

1.1 Ruins of Episcopal mission on the left.

2.2 Return to the parking lot.

Intervals: Vertical, 200 ft; Horizontal, .5 mi.

37 Saddleback Mountain

A circuit hike that passes an Appalachian Trail maintenance hut, threads through a forest that is regrowing after decades of farming, and concludes by passing through tangles of large trees toppled by Tropical Storm Fran in September 1996.

Skyline Mile: 62.8
Distance: 3.8 miles, lariat.
Difficulty: Easy to moderate.
Traffic: Light.

Maps: National Geographic Trails Illustrated Topographic Map 228; Map 10, Appalachian Trail and Other Trails in Shenandoah National Park, Central District (PATC, Inc.).

Finding the trailhead: The trail begins at the South River Picnic Area at Mile 62.8 on Skyline Drive. Go to the lower loop of the picnic area to the kiosk for the trailhead to South River Falls. Follow the blue blazes downhill.

The Hike

For those interested in an easy hike that includes the Appalachian Trail in over three-fourths of the trail's length—and for those interested in witnessing the aftermath of violent storms—this trail is for you. In itself, Saddleback Mountain is rather insignificant, for it offers no real views in the spring, summer, or fall. As a result, it's appropriate that the trail simply circles the mountain and returns you to your starting point. This trail, then, makes no spectacular climbs, but near the end, along the AT, this route passes through an area of immense blowdown. The route is somewhat unremarkable and it's

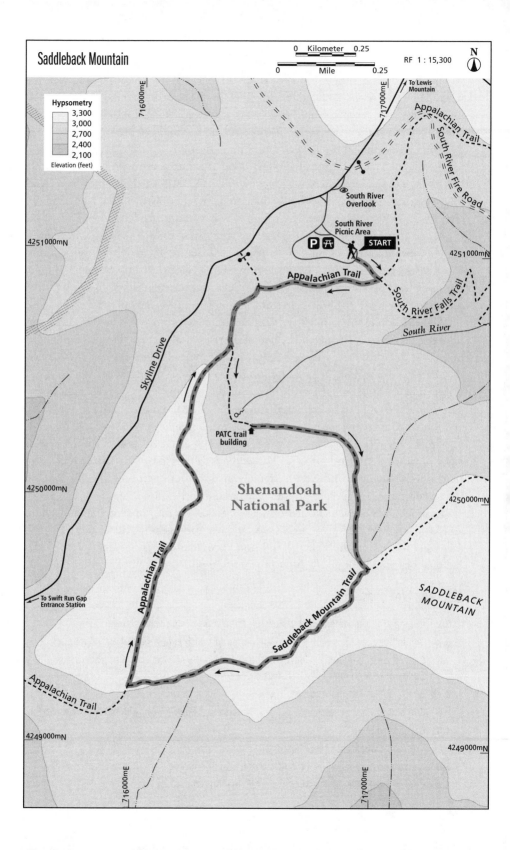

difficult to tell just where Saddleback Mountain is in relation to the hike, but it is a pleasant walk through the woods. For about 0.1 mile the trail threads through an area where blowdown once thoroughly covered the trail. The trail crew has cleaned up the litter, leaving, of course, trees in the woods as they were when they fell. This will give you a good idea of how damaging 70-mile-per-hour winds can be.

The trail begins off the lower loop of the South River Picnic Area, at the kiosk for the trail to South River Falls. Follow the trail's blue blazes downhill for 0.1 mile to a cement post, where there is a junction with the AT. Turn right onto the AT and follow it for another 0.2 mile to a T junction. Turn left; now the AT is part of an old service road. The trail begins to get overgrown, but not nearly as much as farther on.

A canopy of trees obscures the sky, and you can see much new growth following the abandonment of an old settlement. At about 0.5 mile, you see another cement post. Bear left onto a very overgrown old service road. For the next 0.3 mile, this fairly level portion remains overgrown. Use caution; when wet, the path can be slick. You'll soon see the blue blazes of the Saddleback Mountain Trail on the trees.

About 0.8 mile from your start, you encounter what once was an AT shelter but now is a PATC maintenance hut. There is a fire pit and picnic table, but camping is not allowed. To the left, a fairly large spring sits at the edge of a somewhat open meadow. Continue past the building (on the right) and straight ahead on the blue-blazed trail. A slight ascent begins here, and the terrain becomes even more overgrown. Carpets of ferns line the trail. You begin to see the blowdown along the trail, and the scene increases in drama as the trail winds gently upward.

Cross a tiny creek at about mile 1.8, then reach a cement post at mile 1.9. Turn right onto the AT (north) and, still ascending, follow the white blazes through a tremendous blowdown; note the extremely shallow root systems of these huge trees. (From this point, it's another 1.9 miles to complete the loop.)

At mile 3.3 you reach another cement post. Stay on the AT by going left (still on an old road). In 0.2 mile you encounter another cement post. Go to the right, still following the AT north. Near the end, you encounter one last cement post. Follow the blue blazes straight up the hill to the starting point and completion of the loop.

Miles and Directions

0.1 Turn right at the cement post. Follow the Appalachian Trail (white blazes).

0.3 Cement post at T junction. Go left, still on the AT, which is now part of an old road.

0.5 Cement post. Bear left, no longer on the AT but on the service road that leads to the Saddleback Mountain Trail (blue blazes).

0.79 Spring on the left—hard to see.

0.8 South River PATC maintenance building. No camping. Walk straight with building on your right.

1.0 Begin ascending.

1.8 Tiny creek, which may be almost dry.

1.9 Cement post. Junction with the AT. Go north (right). Ascend.

3.3 Cement post. Stay on the AT by going left, still on old road.

Intervals: Vertical, 100 ft; Horizontal, 1 mi.

3.5 Cement post. Go right, still following the AT.

3.7 Cement post. Follow blue blazes uphill.

3.8 Complete hike.

38 South River Falls

An enjoyable hike to the park's third-largest waterfall.

Skyline Mile: 62.8
Distance: 4.4 miles out and back.
Difficulty: Moderate.
Traffic: Light.

Maps: National Geographic Trails Illustrated Topographic Map 228; Map 11, Appalachian Trail and Other Trails in Shenandoah National Park, South District (PATC, Inc.).

Finding the trailhead: The trail begins at the South River Picnic Area at Mile 62.8 on Skyline Drive.

The Hike

At 83 feet, South River Falls is the park's third-largest falls. A refreshing pool at its base would be invigorating on a hot summer day—all the better to prepare you for the challenging hike back to the trailhead.

The trailhead to South River Falls is to the right of the drinking fountain at the picnic grounds at Mile 62.8 on Skyline Drive. The trail descends gradually for 0.1 mile to a junction with the Appalachian Trail. A cement post orients you to the surrounding features. Milam Gap and Swift Run Gap are 11.5 miles and 3 miles to the southwest, respectively.

Continue your hike from the post. You begin a series of gradual switchbacks as you descend the trail. In places the trail is rocky, but it is wide and, for the most part, smooth until it approaches the first of several creeks that combine to create the South River. In the past, hikers have attempted to save time by cutting across the trail, creating erosion. As a result, the park stipulates via several signs that hikers remain on the trail.

South River Falls

N

RF 1 : 11,600

0   Kilometer   0.25

0   Mile   0.25

Shenandoah
National Park

Appalachian Trail

South River Fire Road

South River Falls Trail

South River Falls

View base
of falls

South River

South River

Skyline Drive

To Big
Meadows

South River Overlook

South River Picnic Area

P

START

To Swift
Run Gap

Appalachian Trail

4251000mN

717000mE

718000mE

4251000mN

718000mE

717000mE

Hypsometry

3,300
3,000
2,700
2,400
2,100
1,800
1,500

Elevation (feet)

At 0.75 mile you encounter another creek entering from the left. It's difficult to see because it runs beneath the rocks, but it certainly is audible. Just past the creek lie a number of trees downed by the strong winds of the 1996 tropical storm, Fran. Other creeks continue to flow from the left into the South River, which parallels the trail as it continues its descent.

Intervals: Vertical, 400 ft; Horizontal, 1 mi.

At about 1 mile the trail plunges dramatically downward into a great hollow. It is difficult to see the falls until you approach a natural overlook, located 1.3 miles from the trailhead. Don't get too close to the edge. A few yards farther along the trail, cement walls provide a more protected spot from which to view the falls below you.

At this point, you may turn around and retrace your steps, making this a 2.6-mile hike. If you have the time and energy, continue to the base of the falls for a journey of 4.4 miles.

If you continue, the trail will join an old road that comes in from the left in 0.2 mile. It leads to the South River Fire Road. However, continue along the widening South River Falls Trail, which was once used by inhabitants traveling from one hollow to another. This wider trail descends for 0.6 mile and then swings back toward the base of the falls and a cement post encircled by an aluminum band. The post states that it is 0.3 mile to the end of the road and the park's boundary with the Virginia Wildlife Management Area. It also advises you of the existence of a short spur trail to the waterfall's base about 0.1 mile away. Take the narrow spur trail. You may have to scurry over downed trees.

Alternative hike 38a: For yet another 4.7-mile hike, retrace your steps from the falls. In 0.7 mile you come to the trail junction where a cement post offers an alternative route back to the South River parking lot by turning right onto the old road. Go 0.4 mile to the yellow-blazed South River Fire Road and turn left. Go 0.8 mile to the Appalachian Trail (white blazes) and turn south (left). Go 0.5 mile to a cement post at a four-way junction; turn right onto the South River Falls Trail. It's now 0.1 mile back to the parking lot.

Miles and Directions

0.1 Cross the Appalachian Trail and continue descent on the South River Falls Trail.

1.3 Overlook for South River Falls.

1.5 Junction with old road.

2.1 Path from trail to spur trail.

2.2 Spur trail to South River Falls. Retrace your steps from here.

4.4 Trailhead.

South District
Skyline Mile 65.5 to 105.4

The South District offers an abundance of panoramic views and interesting place names such as Hightop, Rockytop, and Rocky Mount. The South District also has its share of spectacular falls and several designated wilderness areas.

Access to this portion of the park is relatively easy. The South District begins at Swift Run Gap in the north and ends just north of Waynesboro, Virginia. U.S. Highway 33 runs through Swift Run Gap on the northern edge of this section between Stanardsville and Harrisonburg.

Rock scrambling on Hightop in the South District. ▶

South District Overview

RF 1 : 263,900

N

Shenandoah

Harrisonburg

Elkton

To Lewis Mountain

Swift Run Gap Entrance Station

Grottoes

Shenandoah

National Park

Loft Mountain

Skyline Drive

To Blue Ridge Parkway

Rockfish Gap (South) Entrance Station

To Charlottesville

Hypsometry

4,000
3,000
2,000
1,000
0

Elevation (feet)

39 Hightop Mountain Lariat

This is a moderately easy climb to the summit of the highest point in the park's South District with magnificent westerly views.

Skyline Mile: 69.9
Distance: 3.6 miles, lariat; 4 miles with spur trail.
Difficulty: Moderate.
Traffic: Light.

Maps: National Geographic Trails Illustrated Topographic Map 228; Map 11, Appalachian Trail and Other Trails in Shenandoah National Park, South District (PATC, Inc.).

Finding the trailhead: Park at Smith Roach Gap at Mile 69.9 on the east side of Skyline Drive. At a cement post in the parking lot, access the Smith Roach Gap Fire Road for about 10 yards to another cement post indicating the Appalachian Trail junction. Turn north (left) onto the AT; follow the white blazes.

The Hike

Hightop Mountain is the highest peak in the park's South District. It is possible that John Lederer, the noted German explorer, reached the area in 1669. The hike begins at the Smith Roach Gap parking lot (2,620 feet).

Because the trail ascends so gradually, the entire trip should take about three hours. The lot can accommodate only a small number of vehicles, so if it is full (unlikely), choose an alternative hike. Begin your hike at the fire road and follow it for about 10 yards, at which point it intersects the Appalachian Trail. Go north (left), following the familiar white blazes.

The trail begins in a hardwood forest and switches back and forth as the trail begins a gradual ascent. The trail is not rocky and continues as an easy to moderate hike for the first mile. Flanking the trail is an old field that once was used by local inhabitants who farmed the area about sixty years ago—time enough for pioneer vegetation to take hold but not long enough for the resurgence of a mature forest. Still about a mile from the trailhead, the trail begins to level, and at 1.2 miles you will encounter a cement post. The summit is 0.6 mile farther. Continue straight on the AT, crossing the fire road. In 0.1 mile you might want to follow the spur trail to the Hightop Hut.

The hut sleeps about eleven hikers, who need permits for two nights or more. (If the hut is full, you can sleep in a "designated campsite" under the stars nearby.) The Potomac Appalachian Trail Club (PATC)

Intervals: Vertical, 200 ft; Horizontal, 1 mi.

The view from Hightop Mountain.

provides a log book, and it is inspiring as well as amusing to read the entries made by AT hikers. Many make mention of the overabundance of aggressive mice. It would seem that almost all AT hikers take an alias for the trek, with signatures in the book including names such as "Tadpole," "Earthsurfer," "Purple Haze," "Grin-and-Bear-It," "Rusted Boot," and so on.

Backtrack to the AT north from the hut and continue the climb to the summit of Hightop. The peak is designated by a cement post, but you must continue for about 25 yards to an overlook on the left that provides sweeping views to the west, southwest, and northwest as well as a jumble of boulders that are in themselves worthy of inspection. Near the summit, alder bushes form a canopy over the trail.

On a clear day, you can see Skyline Drive below you, a little to the south of west. Looking west, you can see the Massanutten Mountain Range, once considered as the site for establishment of a national park. Because the overlook is slightly downhill from the summit, views to the east are obscured by vegetation. Take time to study the boulders; it took billions of years to get them where they are.

Your descent can retrace your route, or it can follow Hightop Fire Road to the old Smith Roach Gap Fire Road. In either case, you must descend, retracing your steps along the AT for 0.6 mile. For the sake of variety, we suggest you follow the fire road, which goes left at the cement post near the AT hut (blue blazes). It may add another 0.2 mile but no elevation gain. Assuming you follow our route, go left on the fire road for another 0.6 mile.

Alternative hike 39a: If you'd like a slightly shorter trip up to the Hightop summit, park on the west side of Mile 66.7 on Skyline Drive. Cross the drive to the east side and follow the Appalachian Trail south to the summit, which is approximately 1.4 miles away. Retrace your steps from the summit for an out-and-back hike of 2.8 miles.

Miles and Directions

1.2   Cement post. Trail goes to left on the Appalachian Trail to the PATC Hightop Hut.

1.8   Hightop summit. For panoramic view, turn left at the double white blaze just beyond the cement post. Retrace your steps on the AT going south.

2.4   Cement post. Junction with the Hightop Fire Road. Turn left onto the road.

3.0   Cement post on left. Bear right onto the Smith Roach Gap Fire Road toward Skyline Drive.

4.0   Parking lot. End of loop hike. Mileage includes visit to hut.

40 Powell Gap

This is a leg stretcher on the Appalachian Trail that leads to a rock overlook offering excellent views of Powell Gap Hollow and the mountains and farmlands to the east.

See map on page 133
Skyline Mile: 70.0
Distance: 1 mile out and back.
Difficulty: Moderately strenuous.
Traffic: Light.

Maps: National Geographic Trails Illustrated Topographic Map 228; Map 11, Appalachian Trail and Other Trails in Shenandoah National Park, South District (PATC, Inc.).

Finding the trailhead: The trail begins at Mile 69.9 on Skyline Drive at the sign for Powell Gap. Park along the east side of the road near the small meadowlike area.

The Hike

Access the trail by walking to the cement post adjacent to the Powell Gap sign. This hike follows the Appalachian Trail south. It immediately begins to climb, gradually but

Intervals: Vertical, 100 ft; Horizontal, .1 mi.

steadily; it peaks at a short spur trail that provides an overlook to the east. After soaking in the countryside and, if you're lucky, some sun, return to your vehicle.

On a late fall or early winter day, this hike could lead to some spectacular views. This is one of our favorite short hikes.

Miles and Directions

0.5 Rock ledge with great views on your left. Retrace steps.

1.0 Trail's end and your vehicle.

41 Simmons Gap

A short stroll on a historic road that passes the site of an Episcopal mission.

Skyline Mile: 73.2
Distance: 1.6 miles out and back.
Difficulty: Easy.
Traffic: Light.

Maps: National Geographic Trails Illustrated Topographic Map 228; Map 11, Appalachian Trail and Other Trails in Shenandoah National Park, South District (PATC, Inc.).

Finding the trailhead: The trail begins at Skyline Drive Mile 73.2 at the sign for the Simmons Gap Ranger Station. From the south, park on the left (west) side of the road. Cross Skyline Drive and walk down the paved road to the dirt fire road on the right. Begin at the cement post by the yellow chain barring the fire road.

The Hike

The old road descends gently and is marked by yellow blazes and soon parallels a small creek on the right. This stroll follows an old road once used by the mountain people from the east and west valleys to access an Episcopal mission. Later, valley folks used the road for park access. Little remains of this once active area other than an old stone wall.

Today, the Park Service maintains the road as a fire road. Apple trees dot the area, providing mute testimony of a once flourishing agricultural community. A multitude of trees and bushes grace the old road. Near the bottom the trail crosses the creek. A few yards later the trail reaches the park boundary, and you must retrace your route.

Miles and Directions

0.8 Area of old Episcopal mission and park boundary (well marked). Retrace route.

1.6 End of hike.

42 Rocky Mount–Gap Run Lariat

This is one of the park's most difficult wilderness hikes, but one that also provides spectacular views.

Skyline Mile: 76.2
Distance: 9.8 miles, lariat.
Difficulty: Strenuous.
Traffic: Light.

Maps: National Geographic Trails Illustrated Topographic Map 228; Map 11, Appalachian Trail and Other Trails in Shenandoah National Park, South District (PATC, Inc.).

Finding the trailhead: The hike begins at Mile 76.2 on Skyline Drive at a cement post that reads ROCKY MOUNT, just north of Two Mile Run Overlook on the drive.

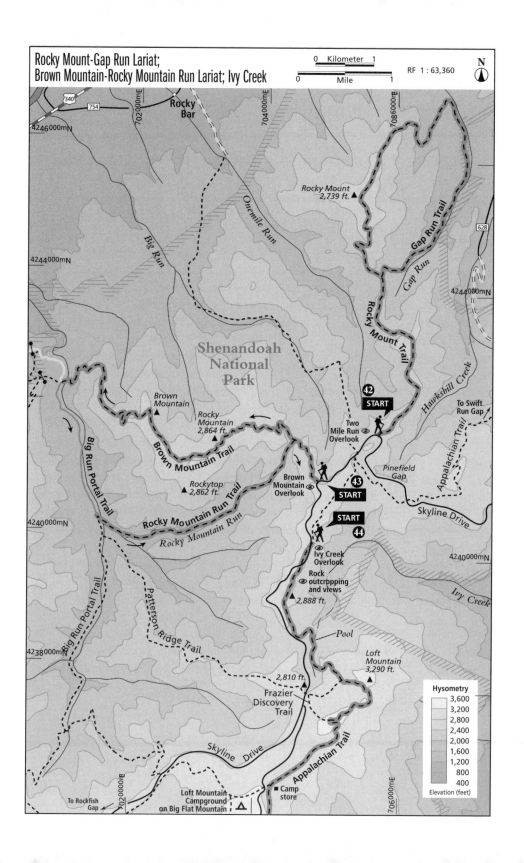

Rocky Mount-Gap Run Lariat;
Brown Mountain-Rocky Mountain Run Lariat; Ivy Creek

0   Kilometer   1

0   Mile   1

RF 1 : 63,360

N

340

754

Rocky
Bar

4246000mN

702000mE

704000mE

706000mE

Rocky Mount
2,739 ft.

Gap Run Trail

628

Onemile Run

Big Run

4244000mN

Gap Run

Rocky Mount Trail

4244000mN

Shenandoah
National
Park

Hawksbill Creek

Brown
Mountain

Rocky
Mountain
2,864 ft.

42
START

Two
Mile Run
Overlook

To Swift
Run Gap

Appalachian Trail

Brown Mountain Trail

Rockytop
2,862 ft.

Pinefield
Gap

Rocky Mountain Run Trail

Brown
Mountain
Overlook

43
START

Big Run Portal Trail

4240000mN

Rocky Mountain Run

Skyline Drive

44
START

4240000mN

Ivy Creek
Overlook

Rock
outcropping
and views
2,888 ft.

Ivy Creek

Big Run Portal Trail

Patterson Ridge Trail

Pool

4238000mN

Loft
Mountain
3,290 ft.

2,810 ft.

Frazier
Discovery
Trail

Hysometry

3,600
3,200
2,800
2,400
2,000
1,600
1,200
800
400

Elevation (feet)

Skyline   Drive

Appalachian Trail

702000mE

To Rockfish
Gap

Loft Mountain
Campground
on Big Flat Mountain

Camp
store

706000mE

Intervals: Vertical, 400 ft; Horizontal, 1 mi.

The Hike

Do not embark on this hike unless you are in excellent shape! However, if you are in good shape, this hike may be just the one for you, particularly if you like remote country that provides a number of spectacular views. At various points along the trail, the abundance of rocks adds to the challenge but also increases the drama and beauty of the area. In addition, the trail proceeds in a roller-coaster–like fashion so that you've ascended many more total feet than the actual 1,600-foot difference between the hike's extreme high and low. For example, the elevation at the trailhead is 2,800 feet while the low is 1,200. Rocky Mount's elevation is 2,739 feet and to reach it you descend, climb, descend, climb, and descend again before climbing back to the trailhead.

Park at Two Mile Run Overlook (Mile 76.4) and walk north along Skyline Drive to the trailhead (Mile 76.2), which will be on your left. The trail crosses back and forth over a ridge, climbs gradually, and descends to its intersection at mile 2.2 with the Gap Run Trail. What goes down must go up, and whether you proceed counterclockwise or clockwise along what, from here forms a loop, is up to you. On the day we hiked, the temperature was cool and we wanted to remain in the sun, so we proceeded counterclockwise. On another day, you might want to proceed clockwise to avoid the sun's intensity.

The Gap Run Trail descends rather abruptly, dropping several hundred feet almost immediately. The descent become a little less intense as it encounters Gap Run, which it crosses about 4 miles from the trailhead. At 4.4 miles from the trailhead, the trail rejoins the Rocky Mount Trail. The trail climbs and does so very abruptly, ascending from a low of 1,200 feet at Gap Run to a high of 2,739 at Rocky Mount, 6.4 miles from your starting point. The trail descends from Rocky Mount, dropping—but then climbing—where, eventually, the Rocky Mount Trail culminates at an elevation of 2,000 feet as it intersects the Gap Run Trail. Along the way, take time to enjoy views of Two Mile Ridge, just beyond Two Mile Run, also in the distance.

Shortly thereafter, the trail begins to climb, intersecting at mile 7.6 with the Gap Run Trail. You're on familiar ground, and so you know you have 2.2 miles more of climbing yet to accomplish to complete the 9.8-mile loop.

Miles and Directions

2.2 Intersection at cement post of the Rocky Mount Trail with the Gap Run Trail. Either turn right onto the Gap Run Trail and begin a steep descent (or stay left on the Rocky Mount Trail if hiking the loop clockwise).

4.4 Northern junction of the Rocky Mount and Gap Run Trails.

6.4 Rocky Mount.

7.6 Southern intersection of the Gap Run and Rocky Mount Trails. Continue right following the Rocky Mount Trail.

9.8 Trailhead.

43 Brown Mountain–Rocky Mountain Run Lariat

A hike across two mountain peaks, dropping down to cross the park's largest stream.

See map on page 135.
Skyline Mile: 76.9
Distance: 10.1 miles, lariat.
Difficulty: Strenuous.
Traffic: Light.

Maps: National Geographic Trails Illustrated Topographical Map 228; Map 11, Appalachian Trail and Other Trails in Shenandoah National Park, South District (PATC, Inc.).

Finding the trailhead: Park at the Brown Mountain Overlook, just north of Mile 77.0 on Skyline Drive. Look for the cement post marking the Brown Mountain Trail (blue blazes). Access the trail in the opening in the stone wall at the Brown Mountain Overlook. Descend.

The Hike

Hikes through this portion of the park not only offer extraordinary views but also provide glimpses into the park's geological past. Along Brown Mountain, sandstone is embedded with 500-million-year-old fossil worm holes. Below Brown Mountain, fire engulfed the area in 1986, and today's hikers have the opportunity to observe firsthand just how quickly nature can regenerate herself. Carry plenty of water, especially in summer.

The trail begins in a relatively open and dry site in the midst of a field of raspberries and begins to descend almost immediately. Within 0.7 mile you encounter the first cement post. Aluminum bands herald the return of the Rocky Mountain Run Trail from the left, but you remain on the Brown Mountain Trail, going right. Shortly thereafter the trail switchbacks several times as it begins to climb, soon reaching a knob. At about mile 1.6 you reach the trail's first exposure, which offers views of Rockytop Ridge and Patterson Ridge. Between them is Big Run Portal

Intervals: Vertical, 500 ft; Horizontal, 1 mi.

where, in the mid 1980s, a hiker ignited a fire while preheating a campstove on a dry and windy day. The fire eventually burned 4,500 acres.

The trail drops and switches back and forth, at times becoming exceedingly rocky. Vines encroach along the trail's flanks. Where the trail is rocky and flanked with vines, its very appearance suggests snakes. Just a few tenths of a mile later, the vegetation changes composition. In August ripe blackberries weigh heavily on branches and stems. It's hard to imagine better bear country and, as we hiked, we found that at least one such omnivore had left its calling card.

About 3 miles along, the trail traverses the right side of the ridge and cuts hard into the side of the mountain, creating a small rock cliff. Trail maintenance here is good, but not excellent.

At about mile 3.8 the trail encounters a talus slope that spans almost 75 yards. The trail soon switches out of the rocks and into a clearing, which offers a great view of Rockytop—not far away as the crow flies. A rock promontory provides the view, which also looks down on Big Run Portal. The trail continues its general downward course and, in a stretch where rocks dominate, may be difficult to find. Look before moving ahead. Look for the familiar blue slash, one of which is on the rocks at foot level.

The trail continues its drops, switching no fewer than six times. As you progress, you'll see charred stumps, mute testimony of the fire that raged through here. Next to it, however, is much new growth, which serves to recall the resiliency of nature. Just before reaching the low point of this loop hike (which you can see as you progress downward), the rocks across the valley containing Big Run Portal appear as palisades. They are prominent and form the base of Rockytop Mountain.

At 5.3 miles, just as you reach the low point of the Brown Mountain Loop, you encounter the junction with the Big Run Portal Trail. Go left. In another 25 feet, you encounter another cement post. This points back toward the Brown Mountain Trail and ahead to the Rocky Mountain Run Trail, 1.4 miles away. The trail is level, more or less, as it crosses Big Run Portal and several feeder streams. Campsites abound. We encountered several backpackers who had been attracted by the opportunity to fish.

At a distance of about 6.7 miles from your point of origin, you again cross Big

Run Portal. Although the stream has diminished in size, it is still substantial. Large boulders have cleaved the stream, creating two beautiful pools and providing an ideal picnic site and several good holes for fishing. Nearby a cement post officially marks your mileage. Turn left at the cement post and take the Rocky Mountain Run Trail, which soon begins to climb. If you had proceeded in the other direction (don't), you'd encounter the Patterson Ridge Trail in 0.2 mile.

As your trail climbs, you cross a feeder stream several times, which in late summer may run beneath the ground and be only a trickle. Often, however, enough water remains to form substantial pools. About 7.5 miles from your point of origin, you see the power of the wind. Off to the left dozens of toppled trees intertwine over the creek, the result of the strong winds of 1996.

At about mile 8.4 a 3-foot-high rock signals a switchback. The trail switches back and forth until you reach a cement post at mile 9.4. You're on familiar ground here, and your point of origin is 0.7 mile away.

Miles and Directions

0.7 Cement post. Remain on the Brown Mountain Trail.

1.6 Views of Rockytop and Patterson Ridges. Trail becomes rocky.

2.2 Rocky Mountain peak on right. Views. Begin to ascend Brown Mountain.

3.1 Descend from Brown Mountain. Views. Steep descent.

5.3 Cement post marking the junction of the Brown Mountain and Big Run Portal Trails. Turn left. Follow yellow blazes.

6.7 Cement post. Turn left onto the Rocky Mountain Run Trail (blue blazes). Steep ascent.

9.4 Cement post. Turn right onto the Brown Mountain Trail.

10.1 Return to the trailhead at mile 77.0.

44 Ivy Creek

A one-way hike containing some moderate and a few strenuous segments that concludes at the Loft Mountain Campground.

See map on page 135.
Skyline Mile: 77.5
Distance: 4.8 miles, one way, shuttle required.
Difficulty: Moderate to strenuous.
Traffic: Moderate.

Maps: National Geographic Trails Illustrated Topographic Map 228; Map 11, Appalachian Trail and Other Trails in Shenandoah National Park, South District (PATC, Inc.).

Finding the trailhead: Ivy Creek Overlook, Skyline Drive, Mile 77.5. Access the Appalachian Trail south from the south end of the parking lot at the cement post (white blazes).

The Hike

Let's say members of your group are tired of hiking and that they hanker to spend the day in camp relaxing. Nevertheless, someone would be willing to drive a short distance and help with your logistical dilemma. What that means to you, the hiker, is that someone can make a fifteen-minute drive and you can walk back to the campground on your own schedule, or they could meet you at the store/dining area on Skyline Drive at Mile 79.5. If that's your situation, consider one of the long hikes described below. If that's not the case, read this section anyway since you can still make the delightful out-and-back alternative hike summarized at the end of this narration. The "Miles and Directions" section below delineates the distances for one-way hikers who want to conclude at the campground. Regardless, all will pass a variety of the park's delights—some (the logistically unencumbered) more than others.

The hike begins from the south side of the Ivy Creek Overlook and immediately provides you with access to the Appalachian Trail. The trail begins with a slight descent amid sassafras, laurel, oak, and pine. The trail begins to ascend, then makes several switchbacks, passing by several large boulders. The trail continues its climb, providing beautiful views to the east of Loft Mountain. In late summer the trail is flanked by mint, goldenrod, and yellow daisies. In the winter the trail is open and spacious and provides unending views.

At 0.7 mile the trail reaches an opening and offers views of Skyline Drive below. Continuing, the trail drops and is flanked by blueberries a species the bears love, as one terrified couple reminded us.

As the trail continues its descent, you can hear the gurgle of Ivy Creek, which soon appears from the left. At 1.4 miles from your point of origin, you cross the creek (but not until after lingering at this delightful spot) and begin a 0.75-mile climb. Along the way the trail parallels the creek—the only place in the park where the AT parallels a stream for any considerable distance. Enjoy!

At mile 2.4 the AT meets an access trail descending to Skyline Drive, as noted by a cement post. Turn left on the AT and continue the climb up Loft Mountain, which periodically offers views of the surrounding countryside.

Intervals: Vertical, 200 ft; Horizontal, 1 mi.

At mile 3.2 the AT reaches a cement post and the summit of Loft Mountain. The right-hand fork at the summit drops down to the Frazier Discovery Trail. Continue along the AT, which descends, and then, once again, begins to climb and continues to do so. At 4.5 miles the trail passes the Loft Mountain camp store, then 0.3 mile later the trail concludes at the campground.

Alternative hike 44a: Perhaps the nicest portion of the Frazier Discovery Trail is the portion of it that drops downhill from Loft Mountain, for that portion of the hike passes by one of the park's more spectacular overhangs. From mile 3.2 on the Ivy Creek hike (above), proceed down the Frazier Discovery Trail, which takes you back to Skyline Drive. The Loft Mountain camp store is 0.9 mile up the road across from the wayside, and the campground is 0.3 mile farther.

Alternative hike 44b: For those who cannot resolve the problem of logistics, this hike provides the only alternative—an out-and-back hike from the Ivy Creek Overlook. Proceed as outlined above to mile 1.4, the Ivy Creek Pool. Then retrace your route, climbing back uphill to the overlook for a round-trip total of 2.8 miles.

Miles and Directions

0.0 Ivy Creek Overlook at Mile 77.5 on Skyline Drive. Access the Appalachian Trail south at south end of lot.

0.7 Rock outcropping and views to the west, on right-hand side of trail.

1.4 Ivy Creek and pool.

2.2 Ivy Creek Spring and maintenance building. Stay left on the AT south.

3.2 Cement post. The right-hand fork proceeds down the Frazier Discovery Trail. Continue straight on the AT south.

4.5 The AT passes the camp store.

4.8 The AT passes the Loft Mountain Campground.

Loft Mountain and Other Hikes from the Loft Mountain Complex (Skyline Mile 79.5)

The Loft Mountain Complex offers many amenities to travelers, the best of which are the area's relatively short hiking trails. For ease of reading, we've detailed several of the hikes you might make from the complex and mile 79.5 of Skyline Drive.

From the Loft Mountain Wayside on Skyline Drive, take the road east. Within 1 mile you'll see the camp store and the amphitheater. The Loft Mountain Campground is 0.3 mile farther and is not on Loft Mountain at all but rather on Big Flat Mountain. Camping is on a first-come, first-served basis, with spaces for trailers, RVs, and tents. Walk-in sites are available for tents only. The bathrooms offer flush toilets

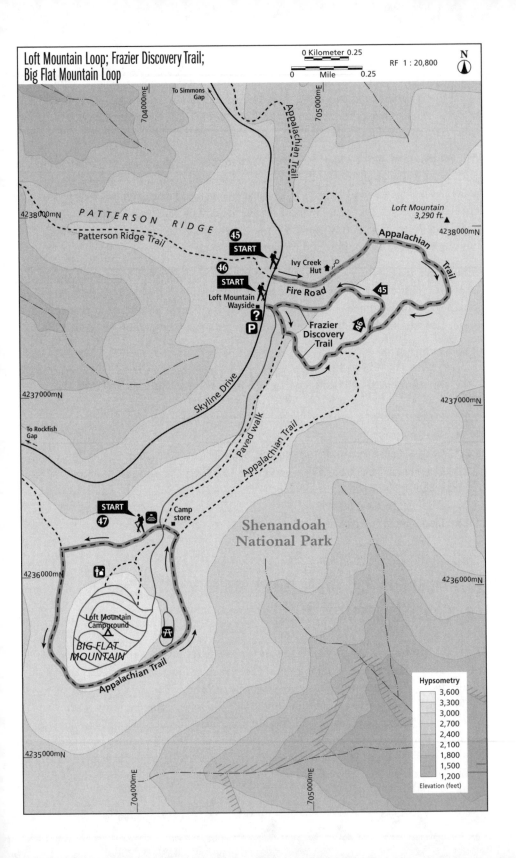

Loft Mountain Loop; Frazier Discovery Trail;
Big Flat Mountain Loop

0 Kilometer 0.25
0 Mile 0.25

RF 1 : 20,800

N

To Simmons Gap

Appalachian Trail

704000mE

705000mE

PATTERSON RIDGE

4238000mN

Patterson Ridge Trail

Loft Mountain
3,290 ft.

4238000mN

Appalachian

45
START

46
START

Ivy Creek
Hut

Fire Road

45

Trail

Loft Mountain
Wayside

?

P

Frazier
Discovery
Trail

46

Skyline Drive

4237000mN

4237000mN

To Rockfish
Gap

Paved walk

Appalachian Trail

START
47

Camp
store

Shenandoah
National Park

4236000mN

4236000mN

Loft Mountain
Campground

BIG FLAT
MOUNTAIN

Appalachian Trail

4235000mN

4235000mN

704000mE

705000mE

Hypsometry

3,600
3,300
3,000
2,700
2,400
2,100
1,800
1,500
1,200
Elevation (feet)

and cold water. The campground makes a good base if you're hiking trails within a reasonable driving or walking radius.

Loft Mountain is the most southern of the park's complexes, and this area was severely damaged by the tropical storm of 1996. The Park Service has worked hard to restore the place and has succeeded. However, you can find ample evidence of the damage in the form of blowdown by hiking backcountry trails in the vicinity. The trails are cleared, though, and in good condition. However, due to the large number of dead trees yet standing, this is one area where you need to assess the forest canopy before camping or picnicking.

45 Loft Mountain Loop

A fun family hike to the northeast summit of Loft Mountain; views offered at several places.

Skyline Mile: 79.5
Distance: 2.7 miles, loop.
Difficulty: Easy.
Traffic: Light to moderate.

Maps: National Geographic Trails Illustrated Topographic Map 228; Map 11, Appalachian Trail and Other Trails in Shenandoah National Park, South District (PATC, Inc.).

Finding the trailhead: Park at Mile 79.5 on Skyline Drive, at the Loft Mountain Wayside parking lot. Walk north on Skyline Drive (you pass the Patterson Ridge Trail on the left) for 150 yards to a dirt road on the right. Follow this road.

The Hike

This is a very enjoyable hike and one that is suitable for a fun family outing.

From the Loft Mountain Wayside parking lot, walk north on Skyline Drive for about 150 yards to a dirt road on the right. Along the way you pass the trailhead for the Patterson Ridge Trail (a one-way trail) on the left. Turn onto the dirt road, walk about 60 yards, and go right again on the dirt road. Soon you'll come to the Ivy Creek PATC maintenance building and Ivy Creek Spring. The Appalachian Trail junction is about 200 yards ahead. Upon reaching the AT, turn right and ascend through the hardwood forest.

As you approach the top, the trees become more widely spaced and blackberry bushes abound. After about 1 mile the trail levels out on the ridgetop. Soon there is an overlook on the left of the trail, with rock outcroppings. Here you'll find lovely 180-degree views to the east of the Piedmont (on

Intervals: Vertical, 50 ft; Horizontal, 1 mi.

clear days); to the left is Flat Top Mountain, and to the right is Fox Mountain with three peaks, a hollow, then two more peaks. The valley below offers pastoral settings, and you can watch clouds and storms roll in. Fields of yarrow (a medicinal plant) and more berry bushes also populate the ridgetop.

At the next cement post you have several options. We turned right onto the Frazier Discovery Trail fork, encountering another great viewpoint on the right. You can follow the Frazier Discovery Trail down to Skyline Drive and the wayside parking lot, or at the cement post at mile 1.4, continue straight on the AT and access the other fork of the Frazier Discovery Trail, thus returning to your starting point. For your third option, continue straight on the AT for another 1.3 miles to the Loft Mountain Campground, if you haven't left your vehicle at the wayside parking lot.

Miles and Directions

60 yards Cement post. Turn right on dirt road. Ascend.

0.4 Cement post. Ivy Creek PATC maintenance building and spring. Follow blue blazes uphill. Cross small creek.

0.6 Cement post. Junction with the Appalachian Trail. Turn right and follow white blazes uphill.

1.0 Trail levels on ridgetop.

1.1 Overlook on left looking northeast to the summit of Loft Mountain. Ascend once again briefly, then cross the saddle to the southwest summit of Loft Mountain.

1.4 Cement post. You have three options: (1) Turn right to return to the wayside via the Frazier Discovery Trail fork. This is the route of our description. (2) Stay straight to access the other fork of the Frazier Discovery Trail and return to the Loft Mountain Wayside. (3) Stay straight on the AT to the Loft Mountain Campground, 1.3 miles farther.

1.5 Side trail to right, leading to overlook.

2.7 Return to Skyline Drive and Loft Mountain Wayside parking lot.

46 Frazier Discovery Trail

A 1.3-mile loop that introduces hikers to discoveries along the trail.

See map on page 142.
Skyline Mile: 79.5
Distance: 1.3 miles, loop.
Difficulty: Moderate.
Traffic: Light to moderate.

Maps: National Geographic Trails Illustrated Topographic Map 228; Map 11, Appalachian Trail and Other Trails in Shenandoah National Park, South District (PATC, Inc.).

Finding the trailhead: The trail begins at Mile 79.5 on the east side of Skyline Drive, on the northern end of the Loft Mountain Wayside parking lot. Look for a cement post marking the Frazier

Overhang on the Frazier Discovery Trail.

Discovery Trail. Access the right-hand fork of the trail. The trail is blue-blazed. You may purchase a guide at the trailhead or at the information center.

The Hike

The Frazier Discovery Trail is a 1.3-mile loop. Pets are not allowed.

The trail begins on the east side of Skyline Drive, immediately to the left of the spur road that departs the drive and begins its climb to the campground. The Frazier Discovery Trail also begins its climb quickly; in other words, you get out of your car and begin climbing immediately (if you choose to take the loop counterclockwise). There's nothing gradual about the climb. But be of good cheer: The climb, though steep, isn't too long. Just watch yourself at first if you are not used to climbing. Take time to rest and absorb the sounds of nature, which are many. On our hike, we were immediately confronted by a catbird that voiced its disapproval of our presence.

In about 0.5 mile a cement post identifies your location, pointing to the Loft Mountain Campground (1.2 miles away), and directs you along your way. Take the Appalachian Trail north (left) and continue up (you're almost to the top) for about 0.1 mile more, which in fact brings you to the summit—and views. All views are made from an extensive rock outcropping that is covered with lichen.

Views from the overlook are commanding, though unidirectional. Because of extensive stands of oak to the east, views in that direction are blocked. However, to the west you can see Skyline Drive threading its way both north and south. You can also see Massanutten Mountain, once a contender for national park status. You can see Hightop to the south. Closer at hand, you invariably see the ever-present vultures circling high overhead, gliding as they search for carrion. Closer yet are stands of laurel, oak, and alder. Equally as important is what you can't see. Below are no towns or cities, and except for Skyline Drive the scene appears very much as it must have appeared in more pristine times.

Continuing, in about 100 yards the trail comes to a junction. To complete this hike, turn left, once again on the Frazier Discovery Trail, which leads to another rock outcropping that offers views similar to those just described. Continue on the Frazier Discovery Trail, which drops rather steeply. About 0.2 mile farther the trail comes to a rock outcropping that towers about 100 feet overhead. The trail passes beneath the outcropping, which offers a breath of cool air, refreshing on a hot summer day.

Finally, just before you reach the trail's end, the forest adds a dense and extensive carpet of ferns to its floor. Several hundred yards later, the trail completes its loop at the fork.

Intervals: Vertical, 100 ft; Horizontal, .2 mi.

Miles and Directions

0.5 Cement post. Go north (left) onto the Appalachian Trail. Turn onto the left-hand trail for a view from the cliff.

0.6 Loft Mountain summit; rock outcropping. Cement post. Take the Frazier Discovery Trail to the left.

1.3 Back to fork in the Frazier Discovery Trail. End of loop.

47 Big Flat Mountain Loop

A short flat hike on the Appalachian Trail that circles the Loft Mountain Campground, with some views.

See map on page 142.
Skyline Mile: 79.5
Distance: 1.8 miles, loop.

Difficulty: Easy.
Traffic: Light to moderate.
Maps: National Geographic Trails Illustrated Topographic Map 228; Map 11, Appalachian Trail and Other Trails in Shenandoah National

Park, South District (PATC, Inc.).

Finding the trailhead: From the Loft Mountain Wayside at Mile 79.5 on Skyline Drive, take the road east, then south toward the Loft

Mountain Campground. The trailhead is at the amphitheater, which is about 1 mile up the road on the right. Access the trail at the cement post just past the kiosk.

The Hike

The Loft Mountain Campground, built in 1964, is actually on Big Flat Mountain, an area that was once pastureland. The Appalachian Trail makes almost a complete circle around the campground and offers views, some quite spectacular, at the beginning of the hike.

Making this trek around the campground is a good leg stretcher for the entire family, besides providing an idea of what the area once looked like. Not only do you get great views to the west, but also the trail wanders through an open forest and, in places, through forests of ferns, providing parklike settings. The Loft Mountain area was hit hard by the tropical storm of 1996, and evidence of the destruction is well documented in the woods.

Three nice day-hike loops are described on the kiosk at the Loft Mountain amphitheater. Study your maps; you'll be able to come up with your own original ideas for longer or shorter hikes in this area. In the meantime, we suggest the following hike.

From the north end of the amphitheater parking lot, take the paved trail toward the amphitheater. After about 30 yards, turn left and go 0.25 mile downhill to a cement post and the junction with the AT. Go left onto the AT and ascend to a saddle. Here you can walk up to the campground, entering at the "A" loop. But stay on the AT; almost immediately, rocky viewpoints are available to the right of the trail. You are looking west and hopefully it is a clear day, because then you can see the Doyles River and watershed. Jones Run is there, too, and both areas contain famous waterfalls.

Continue on the AT through the woods on the soft path. The trek becomes a very enjoyable walk in the woods, a walk even young children will find fun. However, many viewpoints are becoming somewhat obscured by the rapid growth of young trees. There are several places to the left where you can once again access the campground, one of which is at a cement post, but stay on the AT south to the second cement post, which is just below the camp store. Turn left at the cement post and walk uphill 70 yards to the store. Go left in front of the store for about 0.1 mile and you're back at the amphitheater parking lot to complete the loop hike.

Obviously, you can begin and end your hike from any of several points in the campground. The hike described above seems to be a good length for those wanting after-breakfast or after-dinner exercise.

Miles and Directions

30 yards Turn left. Descend.

  0.25 Cement post and junction with the Appalachian Trail. Go left, up the hill.

  0.5 Trail to left to "A" section of campground. To the right begins a series of rocky viewpoints. Continue on the AT south.

  1.0 Cement post indicating another path into the campground. Stay on the AT.

  1.6 Cement post. Turn left. In 70 yards pass the camp store, turn left on the paved walkway going uphill toward the amphitheater and campground.

  1.8 End of loop hike at the amphitheater.

A stream on Big Run Loop Trail.

48 Big Run Loop

A loop trail taking you through the hardwood forest and much park wilderness.

Skyline Mile: 81.1
Distance: 5.8 miles, loop.
Difficulty: Easy to moderate.
Traffic: Light.

Maps: National Geographic Trails Illustrated Topographic Map 228; Map 11, Appalachian Trail and Other Trails in Shenandoah National Park, South District (PATC, Inc.).

Finding the trailhead: Park at the Doyles River parking lot at Mile 81.1 on Skyline Drive, just prior to the Big Run Overlook on the right. Walk across the drive to the Big Run Overlook. Go to the opening in the stone wall—the trail begins to the west. Almost immediately you come to a cement post, indicating you are on the Big Run Loop, marked by blue blazes on the trees.

Big Run Loop; Doyles River Falls and Jones Run

Hysometry

Elevation (feet)
3,600
3,300
3,000
2,700
2,400
2,100
1,800
1,500
1,200
900

RF 1 : 31,000

N

Kilometer
Mile

700000mE
702000mE
4238000mN

Big Run Portal Trail
Big Run

Big Run Loop Trail

Doyles River parking
To Swift Run Gap
48
P
START
Big Run Overlook
49
Doyles River Cabin

Rockytop Trail

RIDGE
Skyline Drive

4236000mN
Madison Run Fire Road
Big Run Loop Trail
48
Doyles River Overlook
Appalachian Trail

49
Browns Gap Fire Road
Doyles River Trail
Upper Doyles River Falls

BLUE
Browns Gap
P
Lower Doyles River Falls

Dundo Group Campground
Skyline Drive
Shenandoah National Park
Doyles River
Browns Gap Fire Road
4234000mN

Dundo Overlook
Appalachian Trail

To Rockfish Gap
P
Jones Run parking

Jones Run Falls
Jones Run
BROWNS

Jones Run Trail
Doyles River
COVE

To VA-629 and VA-810

700000mN
702000mN

Cedar Mountain
3,330 ft.

Intervals: Vertical, 400 ft; Horizontal, 1 mi.

The Hike

After accessing the trail through the opening in the stone wall at the Big Run Over-look, you come to a sign advising you that fishing is permitted in the Big Run area with a Virginia license.

Follow the blue blazes on the trees and begin descending into the forest. You can still catch views of the Shenandoah Valley to the west. Many young chestnuts flank the trail as do several species of maples, white pine, sassafras, and mountain laurel.

The descent continues, crossing at about 1 mile a tiny, barely running creek. At 1.5 miles the trail ascends a small knoll between two valleys. Heading downhill once more, at mile 2.2 you reach a second, larger, gurgling stream, a branch of the Big Run. The forest canopy opens. Minnows dart in the stream. This is a great rest or picnic stop, a respite from the summer heat. Dunk your head and soak your feet.

At mile 3.5, you encounter a four-way intersection. You will also find a cement post here, indicating the trail's intersection with the Big Run Portal Trail. Access the trail to the east (left), marked with a blue blaze. The trail to the right is the Rocky-top Trail. The Big Run Loop Trail levels as it winds along the ridgetop to the next cement post at a T intersection at mile 4.2. The Appalachian Trail intersects and you turn north (left). Cars on Skyline Drive are easily heard now as the drive is only 0.3 mile from this point. The hike to the road is level; cross the drive to continue on the AT, which is up the road a very short distance to your left.

Ascend above the road, then descend to a large rock outcropping. In approximately 0.2 mile, you encounter the Doyles River Overlook offering views to the east. Walk the length of the overlook parking lot to continue on the AT at the north end. Now the path continues with gentle ups and downs to the last cement post. Go left for 70 feet to the Doyles River parking lot and your vehicle.

Miles and Directions

1.0 Cross a tiny stream.

2.2 Cross a second, larger stream, a branch of the Big Run. Reach the cement post 100 yards farther on the trail. Access the yellow-blazed trail to your left (west) to stay on the Big Run Loop Trail. Ascend.

3.5 Cement post marking the intersection of the Rockytop Trail with the Big Run Loop Trail. Turn east (left), continuing on the Big Run Loop Trail (blue blazes).

4.2 Cement post. Junction with the Appalachian Trail. Go north (left) on the AT. Follow the white tree blazes.

4.5 Access Skyline Drive. Cross the road to continue north on the AT.

4.7 Doyles River Overlook with views to the east. Continue to the AT, which picks up at the north end of the overlook.

5.7 Cement post. Turn left onto the Doyles River Trail (blue blazes). Cross Skyline Drive.

5.8 Doyles River parking lot.

49 Doyles River Falls and Jones Run

A long circuit hike to several of the park's most refreshing waterfalls.

See map on page 150.
Skyline Mile: 81.1
Distance: 7.8 miles, loop.
Difficulty: Moderate to strenuous.
Traffic: Light to moderate.

Maps: National Geographic Trails Illustrated Topographic Map 228; Map 11, Appalachian Trail and Other Trails in Shenandoah National Park, South District (PATC, Inc.).

Finding the trailhead: The trail begins at the Doyles River parking area at Mile 81.1 on Skyline Drive.

The Hike

Though this trail can at times be strenuous, it is one of our favorites. The trail passes by three distinctive waterfalls, so start early and plan to end late.

From the Doyles River parking lot, the trail descends, crosses the Appalachian Trail, and continues its descent, passing 0.3 mile from the trailhead a small spring on the left. A few hundred yards later, the trail branches. The left fork proceeds to the Doyles River Cabin. Take the right fork, which is the Doyles River Trail.

At about mile 0.9 the trail crosses the Browns Gap Fire Road. Stay on the Doyles River Trail, which soon crosses, then parallels, the Doyles River until it reaches Upper Doyles River Falls 1.3 miles from the trailhead. A spur trail leads to the base of the 28-foot-high falls and is worth the brief effort.

Continue along the trail, which takes you to 63-foot-high Lower Doyles River Falls 1.5 miles from the trailhead. As the trail continues, it parallels the Doyles River, passing more cascades and spillways.

Upper Doyles River Falls. ▶

Intervals: Vertical, 400 ft; Horizontal, 1 mi.

At 2.1 miles the trail forms a junction with the Jones Run Trail, which you now follow. About 0.1 mile later, the trail crosses Jones Run and begins to ascend. At 2.8 miles the trail takes you to Jones Run Falls, a gathering place for many, as it has a delightful pool, readily accessible near its 42-foot drop.

The trail continues to climb, reaching the Jones Run parking area at mile 4.6. To complete this loop, turn right at the AT, which passes the Dundo Group Camp at mile 5.1. Continue on the AT, passing Browns Gap at mile 5.8. The trail opens to the Doyles River Overlook 1 mile later. After another 1 mile of fairly easy walking, the trail nears its completion, uniting with the Doyles River Trail. Turn left to return to your vehicle.

Alternative hike 49a: For a shorter alternative hike to all of the above-mentioned waterfalls, start at the Browns Gap Fire Road (see "Miles and Directions," below and "The Hike," above), which also provides a parking lot for about a dozen vehicles and picnic tables. This route reduces the route described above by about 2 miles. The Brown family originally built the road as an old turnpike in the late 1700s, and then used it when taking produce from the Shenandoah Valley to Richmond. During the Civil War, Stonewall Jackson used it for troops. Today, it serves as a delightful alternative route that accesses three waterfalls. Like the Doyles River Trail, it descends sharply. It joins with the Doyles River Trail about 0.5 mile above the upper falls. For the remainder of the hike, follow the description along the Jones Run Trail and back up to the Appalachian Trail, where you really save time by concluding your hike 2 miles from the Doyles River Trailhead.

Miles and Directions

0.9 Junction with the Browns Gap Fire Road.

1.3 Upper Doyles River Falls.

1.5 Lower Doyles River Falls.

2.8 Jones Run Falls.

4.6 Jones Run parking. Access the Appalachian Trail north.

5.8 Browns Gap. Stay on the AT north.

6.8 Doyles River Overlook. Remain on the AT north.

7.8 Doyles River parking lot.

50 Austin Mountain–Furnace Mountain Loop

A strenuous but beautiful hike into a rugged wilderness area within the park.

Skyline Mile: 83.0
Distance: 12.4 miles, loop.
Difficulty: Strenuous.
Traffic: Light.

Maps: National Geographic Trails Illustrated Topographic Map 228; Map 11, Appalachian Trail and Other Trails in Shenandoah National Park, South District (PATC, Inc.).

Finding the trailhead: Browns Gap parking area, 0.1 mile north of Mile 83.0 on Skyline Drive. Follow the road at the yellow chain on the west end of the parking area. Descend on the Madison Run Fire Road.

The Hike

The Austin Mountain–Furnace Mountain area consists of a huge expanse of land. Fortunately, many trails exist there. This trek offers solitude and views and is geologically interesting. Because of the area's diversity, a number of possibilities exist. There are long hikes and several short ones. Time will dictate which alternative you ultimately select. The first part of this narration discusses a long day's hike. Under "Alternative hike 50a" we offer another suggestion.

The hike begins 0.1 mile north of Mile 83.0 at the Browns Gap parking lot. Begin by descending the Madison Run Fire Road at the west end of the parking lot. After 0.8 mile you reach a cement post. Leave the road and go right; this is the Madison Run Spur Trail. Ascend through the forest for 0.3 mile to a cement post where you turn left.

Ascend to a narrow ridgetop that offers splendid views through the trees to both sides. About 0.3 mile later you see a double blue blaze, then a cement post. Go west (left). This is the Austin Mountain Trail. At this point, it is 3.2 miles to the junction with the Madison Run Fire Road. You see prime examples of the damage visited on the oak by the numerous gypsy moths. Because the trees are sparse, lovely vistas open to the southwest. Directly below is Dundo Hollow, and across from it rise numerous mountains, such as Furnace Mountain (2,657 feet).

After about 1.5 miles the descent becomes steep, levels, then drops again and is quite narrow and rocky. Continue to enjoy the great views; just before you drop off the ridge, the farmlands of the Shenandoah Valley come into sight. The trail begins to cross talus slopes. If you look carefully at the rocks you're stepping on, you can see long, indented dark lines, remnants of ancient worms that once bored their way into the sand.

View from Austin Mountain.

At this point you are passing under the summit of Austin Mountain (2,658 feet). The descent becomes radically steep and very tedious due to the many talus slopes and rocks that cross or litter the trail. Amid this terrain, you come to a double blue blaze; the switchback makes a sharp left, then drops down four rock stairs. In fact, the turn approaches 180 degrees, and soon you cross the lower portion of the talus slopes that you crossed above.

About 0.1 mile from the end of the Austin Mountain Trail, you cross a dry feeder stream. Then you pop out onto the Madison Run Fire Road at a cement post. Turn right and follow the Madison Run Fire Road for 0.6 mile—almost to the point where the road crosses a chain and nears one of the park's western boundaries. At this point, you'll see the chain about 0.1 mile away.

Turn left onto the Furnace Mountain Trail. Almost immediately the trail crosses Madison Run, which even in the summer may be a full, flowing stream. A good campsite lies nearby. The trail swings abruptly to the right, parallels the creek for about 100 yards, then turns left and begins to climb—and it doesn't stop climbing.

At about 7.2 miles from this excursion's beginning, the trail reaches a talus slope and continues its climb. At mile 7.7 the trail reaches a cement post directing you to

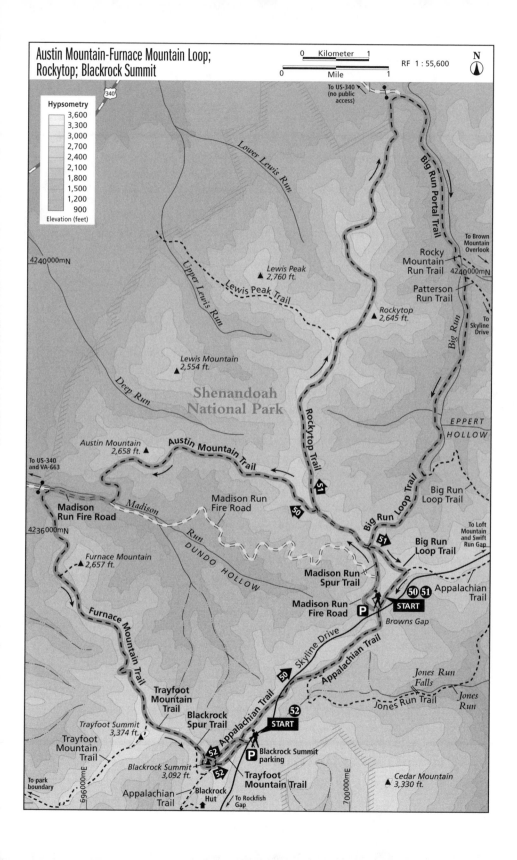

Austin Mountain-Furnace Mountain Loop; Rockytop; Blackrock Summit

Kilometer 1

Mile 1

RF 1 : 55,600

N

Hypsometry

3,600
3,300
3,000
2,700
2,400
2,100
1,800
1,500
1,200
900

Elevation (feet)

340

Lower Lewis Run

To US-340 (no public access)

Big Run Portal Trail

To Brown Mountain Overlook

Rocky Mountain Run Trail

Patterson Run Trail

4240000mN

Lewis Peak ▲ 2,760 ft.

Lewis Peak Trail

Upper Lewis Run

Rockytop ▲ 2,645 ft.

To Skyline Drive

Big Run

Lewis Mountain ▲ 2,554 ft.

Deep Run

Shenandoah National Park

Rockytop Trail

EPPERT HOLLOW

Austin Mountain ▲ 2,658 ft.

Austin Mountain Trail

To US-340 and VA-663

Madison Run Fire Road

Madison Run Fire Road

Madison

Run

DUNDO HOLLOW

51

50

Big Run Loop Trail

Big Run Loop Trail

To Loft Mountain and Swift Run Gap

4236000mN

Furnace Mountain ▲ 2,657 ft.

51

Madison Run Spur Trail

Appalachian Trail

Furnace Mountain Trail

Madison Run Fire Road

P

START

50 51

Browns Gap

Skyline Drive

50

Appalachian Trail

Jones Run Falls

Jones Run

Trayfoot Mountain Trail

Blackrock Spur Trail

52

START

Jones Run Trail

Trayfoot Summit 3,374 ft.

52

P

Blackrock Summit parking

Trayfoot Mountain Trail

Trayfoot Mountain Trail

52

Blackrock Summit 3,092 ft.

52

Appalachian Trail

To park boundary

696000mE

Appalachian Trail

Blackrock Hut

To Rockfish Gap

700000mE

Cedar Mountain ▲ 3,330 ft.

Intervals: Vertical, 500 ft; Horizontal, 2 mi.

the left if you wish to climb Furnace Mountain. If you want to see exceptional panoramas of the area, make the 0.5-mile climb to the top.

Return to the trail after the summit. The main trail continues its climb. If you are ascending on a hot summer day, you'll agree that Furnace Mountain is an appropriate name for the mountain whose flank you are climbing. Much of the trail faces to the southwest, and the length of this excursion makes it difficult to avoid the summer afternoon sun.

The Austin-Furnace Mountains Loop is, in fact, one of the park's more difficult treks. As the trail nears a side shoot of Furnace Mountain, it is covered with rock, making summer hiking even more tiring. Only at a point that approximates your 7.9-mile point does the trail level, but the reprieve is a brief one. In just a few tenths of a mile, the trail again begins to climb.

The Furnace Mountain Trail ends at a junction with the Trayfoot Mountain Trail at a cement post at 9.5 miles. If you turn right, the Trayfoot Mountain Trail will take you to the summit of Trayfoot Mountain, 0.2 mile away, but there is no view. Turn left (east) onto the eastbound fork of the Trayfoot Mountain Trail.

At 10.2 miles the Trayfoot Mountain Trail encounters a cement post. If you turn right, the trail will take you to a point that almost reaches spectacular Blackrock Summit (see Hike 52), from where you follow signs directing you to the Appalachian Trail. The only difference is that you join the AT about 0.5 mile sooner than if you were to climb Blackrock. Remember that your car is still about 2.5 miles away, and that there is yet more climbing to be done.

From the 10.2-mile point, marked by the cement post mentioned above, the trail soon encounters the AT. Take the AT north, passing the Blackrock Summit parking lot. The trail climbs, and about 2 miles later the trail returns you to the Browns Gap parking lot and your hike's end.

Alternative hike 50a: After hiking near the summit of Austin Mountain, traversing as you must the trail's many rocky areas, you may find yourself exhausted or out of time. Fortunately, as you descend onto the Madison Run Fire Road, which you reach at 4.8 miles from your point of origin, you have an option for a 9.1-mile loop. The fire road provides a gradual return to your vehicle along an incline that is fairly gentle. Use the "Miles and Directions" below to take you to mile 4.8 and the intersection with the Madison Run Fire Road. Be sure to carry plenty of water (at least 3 quarts) on this hike, particularly on hot, humid summer days.

After descending from the Austin Mountain Trail, turn left at mile 4.8 onto the Madison Run Fire Road and begin a gradual ascent. Although you are no longer in the wilderness, the boundaries extend to within a stone's throw of both sides of the road. On this part of the hike, we were musing about snakes and bears. Suddenly 30 feet ahead, a large black bear tore from the woods and came to a halt. Jane yelled, "Git," and it got. So much for her fear of bears!

Miles and Directions

0.8 At the cement post go north (right) onto the Madison Run Spur Trail, which leads to the Austin Mountain Trail. Ascend.

1.1 Past the cement post 0.4 mile, access the Austin Mountain Trail, at intersection with Big Run Loop Trail.

1.5 Junction with the Austin Mountain Trail and Rockytop Trail. Go west (left) and continue on the Austin Mountain Trail.

4.8 The Austin Mountain Trail joins the Madison Run Fire Road. Turn right.

5.3 Cement post. Turn left (south) off the Madison Run Fire Road and onto the Furnace Mountain Trail.

7.7 Continue straight, or take the 0.5-mile spur to the top of Furnace Mountain (worth the detour).

9.5 Cement post. Junction of the Trayfoot Mountain and Furnace Mountain Trails. The Furnace Mountain Trail ends. Bear left (east) onto the eastbound fork of the Trayfoot Mountain Trail.

10.2 At the cement post take the left fork of the Trayfoot Mountain Trail to the Blackrock Summit parking area, bypassing Blackrock Summit (if you wish) and picking up the Appalachian Trail north just before the Blackrock Summit parking lot. Continue on the AT for about 2 more miles.

12.4 Browns Gap parking area. End of loop.

51 Rockytop

A ruggedly beautiful all-day hike (or backpack) on Rockytop's ridges, crossing Big Run many times.

See map on page 157.
Skyline Mile: 83.0
Distance: 14.7 miles, loop.
Difficulty: Strenuous.
Traffic: Light.

Maps: National Geographic Trails Illustrated Topographic Map 228; Map 11, Appalachian Trail and Other Trails in Shenandoah National Park, South District (PATC, Inc.).

Finding the trailhead: Browns Gap parking area, 0.1 mile north of Mile 83.0 on Skyline Drive. Take the Madison Run Fire Road at the chain in parking lot.

The Hike

Rockytop and the country through which this hike courses can best be appreciated by driving to the overlook at Mile 81.2 (Big Run Overlook) and studying the interpretive sign at the overview. The sign summarizes the significance of the watershed, which really is a detail of the topography over which the trail progresses. Note Rockytop Ridge. Note Big Run and Big Run Portal. Note as well the magnitude of the country. That's where the trail courses for 14.7 miles. That's where the trail drops from Rockytop Ridge down toward Big Run Portal and then back up through Big Run. Along Big Run the trail crosses back and forth over several creeks no fewer than half a dozen times.

Waters that course along these streams provide some of the park's best trout fishing. These creeks flow generally toward the east and then north, where they collect to form the South Fork of the Shenandoah. They continue their northern course, eventually merging with other waters to form the Potomac. The South Fork flows around the northern portion of Shenandoah National Park where it joins the North Fork of the Shenandoah just north of Front Royal. The Shenandoah River joins the Potomac River at Harpers Ferry, West Virginia, where the combination then flows southeastwardly, eventually into the Chesapeake at a point about midway between Washington, D.C., and Norfolk, Virginia. As the sign says, the waters of the Shenandoah may be the least appreciated of all the park's features.

Over the course of our trek past Rockytop and down into the land of the Big Run Portal, thunder gods growled at one another along Rockytop Ridge while rain beat out a staccato rhythm on the walls of our tent. During our two-day venture, more than a dozen deer watched from the trail's edge as our muffled footfalls carried us past them.

Much of the area has been designated as wilderness, and in places camping opportunities abound. If you can afford the time, make this a multiday backpacking trip.

Though some prefer to hop onto the Appalachian Trail immediately at the Browns Gap parking lot, to minimize repetition almost completely, we opted to begin our trek by descending the Madison Run Fire Road. From the parking lot, descend this road for 0.8 mile to the Madison Run Spur Trail. Turn right onto the spur trail, which climbs to the Rockytop Trail, which you stay on for the next 0.3 mile. After accessing the Rockytop Trail, watch for trails to Austin Mountain and for the Lewis Peak Trail.

Intervals: Vertical, 500 ft; Horizontal, 1 mi.

Hiking the ridge to Rockytop is inspiring. The trail courses back and forth across Rockytop Ridge, sometimes offering northerly views, sometimes southerly. Because the density of vegetation changes, sometimes the views only hint at the area's grandeur, though often they make bold statements. At mile 3.7 the trail passes the Lewis Peak Trail.

Rockytop is 6.3 miles from the trailhead, but things start to happen before reaching the summit. Along the way, the land becomes more rocky and, frequently, talus slopes course down the hill, cutting wide swaths across the trail. Considering the size of the boulders, trail maintenance is excellent and originally must have demanded much ingenuity on the part of the old CCC boys. In places, the trail has been fortified on the downhill side with boulders intended to restrain the downward progression of other rocks and boulders.

Near the summit of Rockytop, a long talus slope becomes part of the trail. The slope stretches for close to 100 yards. Rocks here, and along much of the way, are sandstone in origin, and it is here that the ancient sea worm once made its home.

At places along the ridgecrest (near Rockytop) trees may have toppled. Imagine what the wind can do here, and then you know why the trails may not be as clear as elsewhere in the park. Just below Rockytop, the berries can be as thick as the filling in Grandma's blueberry pie. The black bears know it, and should you encounter one dining on nature's bounty, the prevailing advice regarding these bears is to stand your ground. They generally retreat.

The trail passes through the patch and quickly begins a descent of approximately 2.5 miles. Shortly thereafter the trail passes onto an old fire road and about 1 mile later (at 8.8 miles from the trailhead), the old fire road crosses an old steel bridge. On the other side of the bridge, a cement post resides where you must turn right. The trail crosses and recrosses Big Run and several other creeks no fewer than half a dozen times. These crossings are made over the course of the next 4 miles.

When we made our first crossing, rain poured, but all along Big Run large oak trees offered shelter. There are also good campsites throughout the area, so if your weather pattern duplicates ours, consider pitching your tent. Just remember to camp out of sight of others and that you can't build a campfire. Big Run is the very area in which a camper inadvertently started the infamous Big Run Fire of 1986. The fire started in Big Run, spread up the flanks of Rockytop and Rocky Mountain, then ran along Patterson Ridge. Eventually, the fire burned 4,475 acres. More than 500 firefighters battled the blaze.

At mile 12.4 the Big Run Portal Trail joins the Big Run Loop Trail and the easy going is over. Almost all the way back to the trailhead at Browns Gap, the trail ascends. There's no way to avoid it, though perhaps your load is now easier, for presumably you've eaten most of your food and drunk most of your water. So start chugging.

At 13.4 miles from your start, the trail intersects once again with the Rockytop Trail. Turn left and hike 0.7 mile to the AT. At the AT turn south (right) and walk the final 0.6 mile to the trailhead. Much of this is downhill.

Miles and Directions

0.8 Cement post. Turn right onto the Madison Run Spur Trail.

1.1 Cement post. Junction of the Rockytop and Big Run Loop Trails. Go left onto the Rockytop Trail.

1.5 Cement post. Austin Mountain Trail junction. Stay right on the Rockytop Trail.

3.7 Cement post. Junction with the Lewis Peak Trail. Stay right on the Rockytop Trail.

6.3 Approach Rockytop (2,645 feet).

8.3 Cement post. Junction. Go right onto the Big Run Portal Trail. (There is a private road to your left. No public access.)

8.8 Old steel bridge and, on the far side of the bridge, junction of the Big Run Portal Trail and the Brown Mountain Trail. Stay on the Big Run Portal Trail.

11.2 Cement post noting it is 2.3 miles to the Big Run Loop Trail. Intersection with Rocky Mountain Run Trail

11.4 Cement post noting intersection with the Patterson Run Trail.

12.4 Junction of the Big Run Portal Trail with the Big Run Loop Trail, which comes in from the left and which you now follow.

13.4 Crossroads of the Big Run Loop Trail, the Rockytop Trail, and the Madison Run Spur Trail. Turn left onto the spur trail for 0.7 mile to the Appalachian Trail. (You will recognize this junction as the one leading from the Madison Run Fire Road and the spur you took from it.)

14.1 Junction with the AT. Go south (right), following the white blazes.

14.7 Browns Gap parking lot.

52 Blackrock Summit

A short loop hike to a rocky summit with a short boulder scramble at the top.

See map on page 157.
Skyline Mile: 84.8
Distance: 1 mile, loop.
Difficulty: Easy.
Traffic: Moderate to heavy.

Maps: National Geographic Trails Illustrated Topographic Map 228; Map 11, Appalachian Trail and Other Trails in Shenandoah National Park, South District (PATC, Inc.).

Finding the trailhead: The trail begins at Mile 84.8 on Skyline Drive at the Blackrock Summit parking lot on the west side of the drive. Cross the chain and access the old fire road (Trayfoot Mountain Trail) uphill.

The Hike

Once Blackrock was a huge cliff, which cracked thousands of years ago. It tumbled down the mountain's slopes to become the incredible jumble of rocks that awaits you atop the summit. The uneven surfaces are actually the cliff's top. The rocks of Hampton quartzite are covered with dark patches of rock tripe, a variety of lichen.

Blackrock Summit.

In 1781 Thomas Jefferson apparently expressed concern about the safety of Virginia's great seal and the state's archives. Accordingly, Jefferson gave them to a friend who hid them in a cave at Blackrock until the war's end.

The trailhead is located at a sign that interprets the mountain's geology. After acquainting yourself with the area's geology at the trailhead, follow the trail proper uphill for 0.1 mile on the Trayfoot Mountain Trail to the junction with the Appalachian Trail. Take the AT south, following the white blazes. The AT remains level almost all the way to the top—a distance from the junction of about 0.4 mile.

The sight at the summit that greets you as you leave the forest canopy is commanding. Huge jumbles of rocks fall away to form a talus slope to the right of the trail. Meanwhile, more boulders rise sharply to the summit. The trail stops just short of the summit, and to reach it you must scramble a short distance over a maze of boulders. Occasionally, hikers report seeing rattlesnakes sunning themselves on the boulders, so watch where you step.

From the summit you can see Trayfoot Mountain, Horsehead Mountain, Buzzard Rock, and Furnace Mountain. On a very clear day, try to locate Hightop. From the summit, you can access Trayfoot Summit, another 0.7 mile one way. The trail is easy and the remains of an old fire tower greet you, but you get no view.

Intervals: Vertical, 50 ft; Horizontal, 5 mi.

On our hike, we watched biology in action. Toward the end of the trail segment circling Blackrock Summit, a wasp was burrowing into the web spun by a moth, where it began feeding on larvae.

The trail continues following the AT south around the peak to another cement post at mile 0.6. On the post an arrow points left to the old road (Trayfoot Mountain Trail), which leads back to the trailhead and the parking lot.

Miles and Directions

0.0   Blackrock summit parking lot; ascend on Trayfoot Mountain Trail.

0.1   Cement post. Intersect with the Appalachian Trail; take the AT south, following the white blazes.

0.5   Blackrock. Scramble up rocks and boulders to the peak.

0.55 Cement post. The AT intersects with the Blackrock Spur Trail. Continue circling the summit.

0.6   Cement post. Junction of the Blackrock Spur Trail with the AT. Turn left to return to the parking lot via Trayfoot Mountain Trail.

1.0   Trailhead. End of hike.

53 Trayfoot Mountain–Paine Run Loop

A wilderness loop hike passing by Blackrock Summit, ascending Trayfoot Mountain, and crossing a number of beautiful creeks.

Skyline Mile: 87.4
Distance: 9.6 miles, loop.
Difficulty: Strenuous.
Traffic: Light.

Maps: National Geographic Trails Illustrated Topographic Map 228; Map 11, Appalachian Trail and Other Trails in Shenandoah National Park, South District (PATC, Inc.).

Finding the trailhead: The trail begins at Blackrock Gap, Mile 87.4 on Skyline Drive. Access the Appalachian Trail north.

Paine Run. ▶

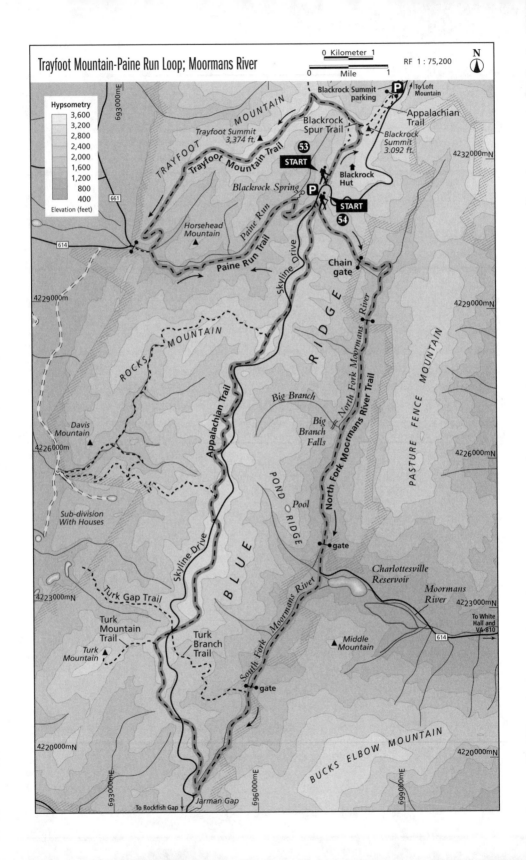

Trayfoot Mountain-Paine Run Loop; Moormans River

0 Kilometer 1

0 Mile 1

RF 1 : 75,200

N

Hypsometry
	3,600
	3,200
	2,800
	2,400
	2,000
	1,600
	1,200
	800
	400

Elevation (feet)

TRAYFOOT MOUNTAIN

Trayfoot Summit 3,374 ft.

Blackrock Summit parking

To Loft Mountain

Appalachian Trail

Blackrock Spur Trail

Blackrock Summit 3,092 ft.

Trayfoot Mountain Trail

53

START

Blackrock Spring

Blackrock Hut

START

54

Horsehead Mountain

Paine Run

Paine Run Trail

Chain gate

661

614

ROCKS MOUNTAIN

Davis Mountain

Appalachian Trail

Sub-division With Houses

Skyline Drive

RIDGE

North Fork Moormans River

North Fork Moormans River Trail

Big Branch

Big Branch Falls

POND RIDGE

Pool

gate

PASTURE FENCE MOUNTAIN

Charlottesville Reservoir

Moormans River

To White Hall and VA-810

614

Turk Gap Trail

Turk Mountain Trail

Turk Mountain

Turk Branch Trail

BLUE

Skyline Drive

South Fork Moormans River

gate

Middle Mountain

BUCKS ELBOW MOUNTAIN

Jarman Gap

To Rockfish Gap

4232000mN

4229000m

4229000mN

4226000m

4226000mN

4223000mN

4223000mN

4220000mN

4220000mN

693000mE

696000mE

699000mE

Intervals: Vertical, 500 ft; Horizontal, 1 mi.

The Hike

This is one of our favorite hikes because it threads through such a variety of land features. Take plenty of water for this hike, particularly if it's a warm day.

This hike begins at Blackrock Gap and climbs and reaches Blackrock at 1.3 miles, where it circles the jumble of rocks forming this spectacular mountain. Views from here are beautiful. At 1.4 miles the trail meets the Trayfoot Mountain Trail and dips between piles of boulders, where it levels for a short distance but quickly begins to climb to the summit of Trayfoot Mountain. After passing the summit of Trayfoot, the trail, which is generally level for about 0.2 mile, progresses along a ridge. The trail begins a sharp descent, passing back and forth across the ridge. About a mile from the summit (3.5 miles from the trailhead), the trail passes by a series of interesting rock outcroppings, then continues its general downhill course.

At 6.2 miles the trail reaches the base of the Trayfoot Mountain Trail where you encounter a cement post noting the trail's intersection with the Paine Run Trail. Almost immediately you cross Paine Run and begin a gradual ascent, crossing a number of feeder streams as you go. At 8.7 miles the trail passes a spur that leads to Blackrock Spring. Often the trail is overgrown and seems to offer a haven for snakes. Bypass the spur and continue climbing along what quickly becomes an obvious road bed and remains such almost until you reach the trailhead at 9.6 miles.

Miles and Directions

0.6 Spur to the Blackrock Hut on the right off the Appalachian Trail north.

1.1 Begin circling Blackrock Summit.

1.2 At cement post halfway around the summit, go left onto the Blackrock Spur Trail.

1.4 Junction with the Trayfoot Mountain Trail. Turn right onto the Trayfoot Mountain Trail.

2.2 Cement post. Go left (southwest) on the Trayfoot Mountain Trail at the junction with the Furnace Mountain Trail, which goes to the right. Ascend summit of Trayfoot Mountain 0.2 mile farther.

2.4 Summit of Trayfoot. Begin descent of about 3.0 miles.

6.2 Cement post indicating the park boundary is 0.3 mile to the west. Turn left onto the Paine Run Trail. Cross creek immediately.

6.4 Cross creek again.

8.7 Intersection with spur trail to Blackrock Spring. Keep right; ascend.

9.6 Blackrock Gap.

54 Moormans River

A fascinating hike departing from Skyline Drive and descending past homesteads to an area at one time ravaged by a "once-in-2,000-years storm."

See map on page 166.
Skyline Mile: 87.4
Distance: 9.4 miles, one way, shuttle required.
Difficulty: Strenuous.
Traffic: Light.

Maps: National Geographic Trails Illustrated Topographic Map 228; Map 11, Appalachian Trail and Other Trails in Shenandoah National Park, South District (PATC, Inc.).

Finding the trailhead: The route begins at the Blackrock Gap parking lot at Mile 87.4 on the west side of Skyline Drive. Cross to the east side of the drive to the cement post and access the North Fork Moormans River Trail (fire road).

The Hike

In 1995 the clouds opened and in a twenty-four-hour period dumped more than 30 inches of rain on portions of Shenandoah National Park. The sudden flood of water over the area affected lives and property. The waters took the lives of eight people and caused millions of dollars in property damage. The effects were felt as well in Shenandoah National Park. Water permeated the ground, and it saturated the soil, which then began to slough. When it did, it carried entire forests, tossing them about like so many matchsticks, and great walls of stone and mud from the hilltops came down like avalanche chutes. Even the trout fishing was adversely affected.

Still, the Moormans River remains an area of much intrigue, perhaps because the damage was caused by nature, not by humans. Park trail crews have invested many hours in restoring the trails. The area is slowly revegetating itself. Though the storm uprooted whole stands of trees, large sycamores still grow along the river. Moormans River is one of the few park areas where this species proliferates.

The trail begins across from the Blackrock Gap parking area and immediately begins to descend along the fire road. What will later become a substantial river is simply a small, almost inconspicuous, stream. Within a mile the stream grows, in part from the several small feeder streams that you must cross. In slightly over a mile, barbed wire begins to flank both sides of the road, suggestive of the considerable private land the fire road parallels. Soon you see posted signs. At mile 1.5 you will see a cattle-loading chute on your left; it's still in use. A hundred yards later, a gate designates private property and a stream comes in from your left. The trail courses through some private property.

At mile 2.1 a chain gate announces your return to Shenandoah National Park. Immediately, the trail crosses a small stream. The trail is obviously still a fire road but one that is not used as much as the upper portion. The trail soon crosses a bridge that may have been washed out by the flood. Just a short distance farther, at about mile 2.3, you encounter your first exposed area of devastation. Above you trees are uprooted in a dramatic fashion—all by a stream that in the summer can at times be dry. At about mile 2.9 the scene repeats itself: Another small stream has significantly altered the landscape. At approximately 3.5 miles, cross Big Branch Run with its 40-foot waterfall and pools 200 yards above the trail.

Just past mile 3.5 the North Fork of the Moormans River begins to swell substantially. No longer is it a trickle; rather it is a significant stream. Almost at the same point, you see an extensive range of cliffs that rise above the river's far bank, which is off to your left.

At 4.7 miles the trail crosses the river and the trail becomes indistinct. You must follow a series of rock cairns that lead you downriver to the trail. About 0.3 mile farther, you encounter another cement post and a sign advising you that you are leaving the park. Continue to the parking area, where you find another cement post located in the center of the lot. The trail is across the river and up on the far bank, which you must climb.

At mile 5.7 a cement post marks the Charlottesville Reservoir parking area. To find the trail, you must rock hop across the stream and climb the bank to the other side of the river.

Your trail continues outside the park, following the South Fork Moormans River Road. As you hike you cross several small streams. At mile 6.35 you wade or rock hop across the South Fork of the Moormans River, now to your right. At mile 7.3 you'll see a well-preserved rock foundation of an old home.

Not until mile 7.5 do you reenter the park. Shortly thereafter, you see an old rock wall that stands 5 feet high in places and 70 to 75 yards wide.

At mile 7.7 you see a cement post that notes the distance to Turk Gap. Continue straight to Jarman Gap, crossing several small feeder streams and passing both a sign

Intervals: Vertical, 500 ft; Horizontal, 1 mi.

warning of the presence of an underground pipeline and another rock wall. At 9.4 miles from your point of origin, the Appalachian Trail crosses your route. Continue straight, concluding your hike at Jarman Gap.

Miles and Directions

0.0 Fire road on east side of Blackrock Gap parking lot.

1.1 Cement post. Cross chain gate. Leave Shenandoah National Park.

1.4 Cement post. Turn right and cross North Fork Moormans River.

2.2 Cross chain gate and note sign announcing entry to Shenandoah National Park. Now on the North Fork Moormans River Trail.

2.3 Area of huge devastation of 1995.

3.5 Cross Big Branch Run.

4.7 Cross the stream and follow rock cairns for a short distance.

5.0 Cross the stream, which is now on the right.

5.1 Beautiful cliffs on the left. On the downstream side of the cliffs, the trail crosses the stream.

5.7 Cement post at center of parking lot. Trail approaches the Charlottesville Reservoir.

6.3 Cross the stream.

6.35 Wade the South Fork (usually quite shallow except in the spring) of the Moormans River, now to the right.

7.2 Beautiful pool.

7.3 Cross the feeder stream. Well-preserved rock foundation of an old home.

7.5 Cement post signifying return to the park.

7.6 Imposing old rock wall.

7.7 Cement post noting the Turk Branch Trail. Stay straight.

9.4 Cement post noting crossing of the Appalachian Trail. Stay straight on the old road to Jarman Gap and the end of the hike.

55 Riprap Trail

This series of trails crosses some of the park's more strenuous, pristine, and inspiring features.

Skyline Mile: 90.0
Distance: 6.7 miles, one way, or 9.8 miles, loop.
Difficulty: Moderately strenuous.
Traffic: Light to moderate.

Maps: National Geographic Trails Illustrated Topographic Map 228; Map 11, Appalachian Trail and Other Trails in Shenandoah National Park, South District (PATC, Inc.).

Finding the trailhead: The trail begins at Mile 90.0 on Skyline Drive at the Riprap parking lot on the west side of the drive. At the cement post, take the Riprap Trail uphill for 50 feet to the Appalachian Trail. Go north (right) on the AT.

Riprap Trail

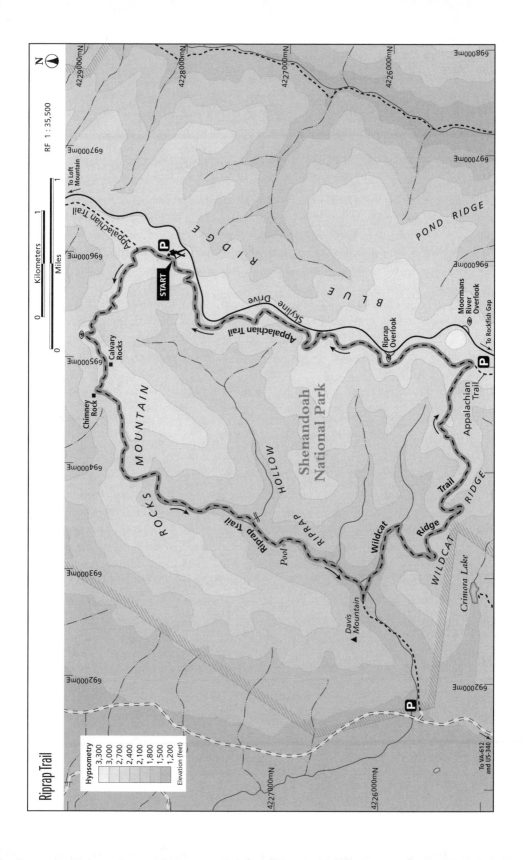

RF 1 : 35,500

Hypsometry
3,300
3,000
2,700
2,400
2,100
1,800
1,500
1,200

Elevation (feet)

The Hike

Wilderness is the theme throughout the trails here. It begins the moment you hit the Riprap Trail just 0.4 mile from the trailhead. It stays with you the entire distance, except for the last mile of the Riprap Trail, where a fingerlike projection of the trail was removed. You quickly reclaim the wilderness as soon as you access the Wildcat Ridge Trail at about mile 4, leaving the wilderness once again when you access the Appalachian Trail at mile 6.7.

Wilderness includes those areas where all permanent evidence of human manipulation of the environment has been removed. When Shenandoah's wilderness was established in 1976, and to comply with the mandates of the 1964 Wilderness Act, one trail shelter was removed. "Today," as the act specifies, "the area contains no permanent evidence that people may once have inhabited the area."

Natural features include ancient quartzite rocks and lofty overlooks from areas where ancient worms once burrowed. As you progress into the wilderness, the area includes long runs created by beautiful streams. It also includes the park's largest pool, where hikers have long made a tradition of overnight treks to bathe and swim on hot summer days.

Many who venture into the area opt to make this an overnight backpacking excursion. The trip is a long one, but well worth every minute you might care to spend. Even if you can't spend days, the trip is well worth the time. The entire loop hike can certainly be made in one day or broken into smaller segments.

This 9.3-mile loop via three trails is a moderate to strenuous hike but one of the prettiest in the park. Within 0.4 mile after reaching the Riprap Trail, for most of the trip you are not only in the backcountry but in designated wilderness. Fishing is permitted with a Virginia license, and you discover backcountry camping spots after the first few miles.

From the end of the parking lot, take the Appalachian Trail north (white blazes), ascending for 0.4 mile under a canopy of oak, maple, and sassafras, to the cement post junction for the Riprap Trail. Go west (left), following the blue blazes. The trail, lined with blueberry bushes, makes a switchback descent, then ascends to a

Intervals: Vertical, 400 ft; Horizontal, 1 mi.

knoll. You come suddenly upon a jumble of lichen-covered rocks and boulders—a jumble known as riprap. At about 0.7 mile you reach a saddle, which provides great views of the Paine Run watershed. The striated boulders are Erwin quartzite, as are the rocks at Calvary Rock and Chimney Rock, not far ahead. Follow the ridgetop up and down to Calvary Rock, at mile 1.4 with a northwest view. Continue another 0.2 mile to Chimney Rock for another view. Iron pegs embedded in the rock are part of an old bridge. For a shorter hike (3.2 miles) retrace your steps from here.

The narrow trail levels, with a couple more small lookout points. It begins a gentle descent off the ridge back into the forest; the downhill trek becomes steeper and rockier.

A tiny, sometimes dry, stream enters from the left but soon becomes wider, flowing freely over rocks. A brown signpost with an arrow indicates that you must stay to the right. It's obvious that the trail has been rerouted here for a short distance. It drops steeply with some rough, rocky parts but is stabilized on the downhill side with rock piles.

At approximately 3.3 miles you must ford the stream by hopping rocks. About 100 yards farther, there's a delightful (and popular) swimming hole on the right. The swimming hole provides a lovely rest and picnic spot. The stream flows in from a wide, gentle incline, and trout inhabit the waters. Across the stream, an old path leads to the former site of the old Riprap Shelter, now removed because of the area's wilderness designation.

Continue down the trail, ford the stream, and arrive at a cement post that provides mileages. Continue on the level but rough and rocky trail with talus slopes on the right.

At the next cement post, at mile 4, turn left (southeast) onto the Wildcat Ridge Trail (blue blazes). Cross another stream almost immediately and parallel it to your left. Cross the stream two more times, then begin the steep ascent to Wildcat Ridge. As you chug ever upward, where the trees begin to thin, you get some sparse views of the ridges to the west.

The trail basically climbs to the next cement post at 6.6 miles. Here you have a choice: If you have two vehicles and have left one (or you have arranged a pick-up) at the Wildcat Ridge parking area, head straight east, following the blue blazes for 0.1 mile to the parking lot, making the entire hike a journey of 6.7 miles. If your vehicle is at the Riprap Trailhead, at the 6.6-mile cement post you must access the AT north (left) for 2.7 more miles, making a hike total of 9.3 miles.

The final 2.7 miles along the AT are not particularly strenuous. The trail combines level hiking with some uphill and some downhill. The AT swings well away from the Skyline Drive and offers occasional views to the west. You see sweeps of rock along the way, areas that the forest is attempting to reclaim. The very last part of the trek swings you around one brief switchback; then you're home.

Miles and Directions

0.4 Join the Riprap Trail from the Appalachian Trail at the cement post. Go west (left, follow blue blazes).

0.7 Saddle, talus slope.

1.4 Calvary Rock, views to northwest.

1.6 Chimney Rock.

3.3 Swimming hole.

3.4 Cement post with mileages. No trail change.

4.0 Cement post. Go southeast (left) onto the Wildcat Ridge Trail.

6.6 Junction with the AT. Go north (left) on the AT to the Riprap Trailhead to complete the loop.

6.7 Wildcat Ridge parking lot and junction with the AT. Go left on the AT if you don't have a vehicle parked there.

9.8 Riprap Trailhead and vehicle by way of the AT to complete the loop.

56 Turk Mountain

An ascent to the inspiring summit of Turk Mountain, followed by a return descent along the same trail.

Skyline Mile: 94.1
Distance: 2.2 miles out and back.
Difficulty: Moderate.
Traffic: Light to moderate, depending on the day of the week.

Maps: National Geographic Trails Illustrated Topographic Map 228; Map 11, Appalachian Trail and Other Trails in Shenandoah National Park, South District (PATC, Inc.).

Finding the trailhead: The trail begins at Mile 94.1 on the west side of Skyline Drive, across the road from the Turk Gap parking area. Take the Appalachian Trail south (left), following white blazes.

The Hike

The trail up Turk Mountain begins across the road from the Turk Gap parking lot, at which point you immediately access the Appalachian Trail south. Continue along the AT for 0.1 mile and turn right onto the Turk Mountain Trail, which follows a brief downhill course, dropping through a saddle. At about 0.4 mile the trail begins to ascend abruptly and continues to do so throughout the climb. Near the top, the trail switchbacks several times, culminating approximately 1.1 miles later at an elevation of 2,981 feet.

Upon reaching what is essentially the trail's end, if you want good views you must scramble over rocks for a short distance. Mountain laurel is edging onto the

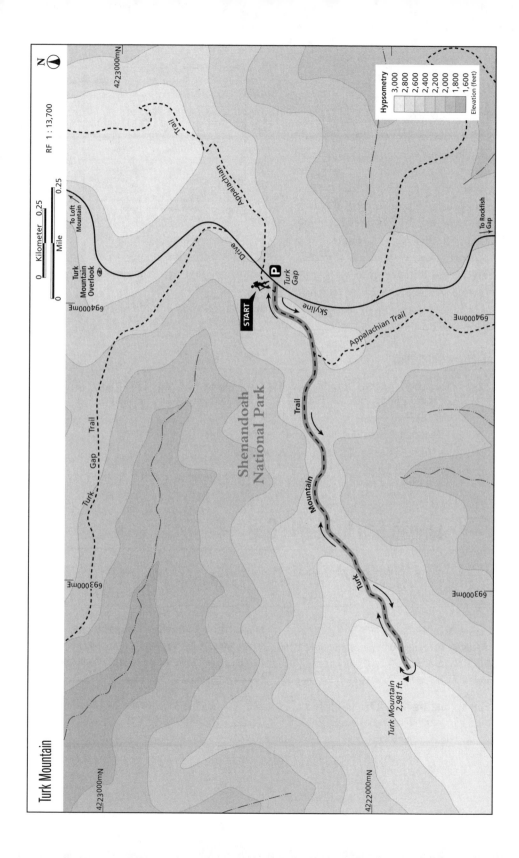

Turk Mountain

RF 1 : 13,700

N

Kilometer 0 0.25

Mile 0 0.25

Hypsometry
- 3,000
- 2,800
- 2,600
- 2,400
- 2,200
- 2,000
- 1,800
- 1,600

Elevation (feet)

Turk Mountain Overlook

To Loft Mountain

Appalachian Trail

Drive

Skyline

START

P

Turk Gap

Appalachian Trail

To Rockfish Gap

Turk Gap Trail

Shenandoah National Park

Mountain Trail

Turk

Turk Mountain 2,981 ft.

6940000mE

693000mE

4223000mN

4222000mN

rocks, but for the most part the scramble is free of slippery vegetation and is well worth the time, not only for the views but also for the geology.

The rocks forming the summit contain mostly quartzite, which the eons and the erosional forces of freezing and thawing have worn down. It is obvious that cataclysmic forces have been at work, for the fractured rocks composing the talus slope spread downward and out for hundreds of yards.

Intervals: Vertical, 200 ft; Horizontal, .5 mi.

Views from Turk Mountain range across the southwestern portion of the horizon. In the distance you can see the Shenandoah Valley, and a bit to the south Sawmill Ridge and Scott Mountain.

The fortunate part of an uphill hike is that the return is downhill. So it is with the rest of this hike.

Miles and Directions

0.0 Cement post. Trailhead. Take the Appalachian Trail south (left), following white blazes. (Do not access the Turk Gap Trail, which intersects from the right and leads to the park boundary.)

0.1 Cement post. Take the Turk Mountain Trail to the right. The AT continues straight.

1.1 Turk Mountain Summit and viewpoint. Retrace your steps.

2.2 Trailhead. End of hike.

57 Jarman Gap to Beagle Gap

A one-way excursion past reminders of mountain people to the summit of Calf Mountain.

Skyline Mile: 96.8
Distance: 2.7 miles, one way, shuttle required.
Difficulty: Moderate.
Traffic: Light.

Maps: National Geographic Trails Illustrated Topographic Map 228; Map 11, Appalachian Trail and Other Trails in Shenandoah National Park, South District (PATC, Inc.).

Finding the trailhead: The trail begins at Jarman Gap on Skyline Drive at Mile 96.8. Access the fire road to the right on the east side of the drive. Go 0.1 mile to the cement post and the Appalachian Trail junction.

Jarman Gap to Beagle Gap;
Bear Den Mountain; Calf Mountain

Kilometer

0   0.5

Mile

0   0.5

RF 1 : 21,600

N

Hypsometry

3,000
2,700
2,400
2,100
1,800
1,500
1,200

Elevation (feet)

Shenandoah
National Park

To Loft Mountain
Jarman Gap

P

57

START

Calf
Mountain
Shelter

R I D G E

Skyline   Drive

4217000mN

Appalachian Trail

4217000mN

Calf Mountain
Overlook

Calf Mountain
2,910 ft. ▲

*MEADOW
AREA*

59

START

B   L   U   E

Beagle Gap

START

P   **58**

4216000mN

Beagle Gap
Overlook

B E A R   D E N   M O U N T A I N

Seats ■

■

■ Towers

4215000mN

Greenwood Hollow

To Rockfish Gap

694000mE

The Hike

From the trailhead, hike 0.1 mile along an old fire road to the Appalachian Trail. Turn right at the cement post onto the AT south and begin a gradual uphill climb. One of the rewards of hiking this trail is the vegetation. As you proceed along the first 0.1 mile, look for the large stands of tulip poplar that grace the woods. You'll recognize the trees by the large leaves with main veins that end in a notch. Tips appear to be cut off.

After encountering the AT, the trail climbs gradually. Within 0.5 mile the trail passes another old fire road, where we found artifacts from an old cabin—old bed springs eroded by the forces of nature. As the Park Service points out, what once was garbage now serves as the pieces in a huge puzzle that cultural anthropologists are still assembling.

Continue on the AT, which soon passes a spring that may be dry in summer. A little farther along, a sign greets you and informs that you are hiking the AT and that it is maintained by the Potomac Appalachian Trail Club. Yet a short distance farther, the trail passes beneath a power line. At 1 mile the trail passes a spur trail that AT hikers often use. The spur provides access to the Calf Mountain Shelter and a spring, located respectively at 0.3 and 0.2 mile along the spur.

As you approach the summit of Calf Mountain, the trail increases in steepness. At one point it switches back and forth and then provides you with a series of wood and stone steps. The rather abrupt incline, however, is short, and within 0.1 mile the trail levels along the summit of Calf Mountain.

The summit of Calf Mountain once served as pastureland, and it's obvious that vegetation is reclaiming the clearing. The trail opens into a parklike setting, and the vegetation consists of sumac, mint, some thistle, and much young pine. In August the raspberries that also flank the trail are ripe.

The trail soon descends, and within 0.1 mile you see more evidence of former human activity: An old stone wall with a width of about 25 yards cuts across the trail. The descent continues through the pasture setting, and as you near the trail's end, an old apple orchard still puts forth a fall harvest. This one-way hike ends on the AT at Beagle Gap.

Miles and Directions

0.1 Cement post. Appalachian Trail junction. Go south on the AT (white blazes).

1.0 Cement post. Calf Mountain AT Shelter and spring on right.

1.7 Calf Mountain Summit.

2.7 Cement post. Trailhead at Beagle Gap, Mile 99.5. End of one-way hike.

Intervals: Vertical, 100 ft; Horizontal, 1 mi.

58 Bear Den Mountain

A leg stretcher to the Bear Den Mountain summit (2,885 feet), offering spectacular views.

See map on page 177.
Skyline Mile: 99.5
Distance: 1.2 miles out and back.
Difficulty: Easy.
Traffic: Light.

Maps: National Geographic Trails Illustrated Topographic Map 228; Map 11, Appalachian Trail and Other Trails in Shenandoah National Park, South District (PATC, Inc.).

Finding the trailhead: The trail begins at Mile 99.5 on the west side of Skyline Drive, across from the Beagle Gap parking area. Go through an iron gate with a white blaze (AT) on a wood post.

The Hike

Walk directly across Skyline Drive (west) from the Beagle Gap parking lot and proceed through the opening in the iron gate with a white blaze on a wood post. Look northwest for views of the Shenandoah Valley.

Following the Appalachian Trail (blazed on rocks), the trail ascends gently through an old meadow. After about 0.2 mile a road intersects the AT; cross it and follow the AT. The ascent leads 353 feet to the summit of Bear Den Mountain. If the day is clear, panoramic views open in all directions. Best of all, seven old tractor seats have been inserted by their posts into the ground, offering thrones on which to perch. The landscape below offers scenery fit for a king or queen.

If you want a slightly longer walk, hike the ridge over to the second set of communication towers. The views are not necessarily better, just slightly different. Retrace the AT back to the parking lot.

Intervals: Vertical, 100 ft; Horizontal, .2 mi.

Miles and Directions

0.6 Summit of Bear Den Mountain. Retrace steps.
1.2 Back at the trailhead and the Beagle Gap parking lot.

59 Calf Mountain

A pleasant hike to the top of Calf Mountain, winding through old pastures and some new-growth trees.

See map on page 177.
Skyline Mile: 99.5
Distance: 2 miles out and back.
Difficulty: Easy.
Traffic: Light.

Maps: National Geographic Trails Illustrated Topographic Map 228; Map 11, Appalachian Trail and Other Trails in Shenandoah National Park, South District (PATC, Inc.).

Finding the trailhead: The hike begins at Mile 99.5 at the Beagle Gap parking area on the east side of Skyline Drive. Walk through the opening in the wire fence with a white blaze on it.

The Hike

This short jaunt up to Calf Mountain is a delightful one, partly because it winds through old meadows and is not a hike through woods. The trail is good for the entire distance, consisting generally of soft dirt rather than rock. In the summer—if it's hot and humid—you might want to make this one early or late in the day. It's also a good walk for frisky children.

Walk through the V opening in the wire fence and ascend through the meadow filled with wildflowers and berry bushes. Entering a small stand of new-growth trees and bushes, the trail quickly becomes a bit steeper for about 0.2 mile. Then you again hike out on the level and into meadows and come upon a large stand of old, still bearing, apple trees.

Intervals: Vertical, 200 ft; Horizontal, .5 mi.

At about 0.7 mile views open to the east. This is not the summit; the top is about 0.3 mile farther. You'll know you have gone over the top when you begin a descent on logs and rocks placed across the trail. From the top, retrace your route and enjoy, once again, the area's openness, its lush vegetation, and its introduced apple orchard.

Miles and Directions

0.0   Beagle Gap parking lot; walk through opening in fence.
0.7   Viewpoint.
1.0   Reach the summit of Calf Mountain. Retrace the Appalachian Trail back to the parking lot.
2.0   Trailhead. Beagle Gap parking lot.

Appendix A: For More Information

The following are excellent sources for hiking and backpacking information, maps, camping and reservations information, books, and other materials concerning Shenandoah National Park.

Shenandoah National Park Headquarters
3655 U.S. Highway 211 E
Luray, VA 22835
(540) 999-3500 (nonemergencies)
For emergencies in the park: (800) 732-0911
www.nps.gov/shen

Shenandoah National Park Association
3655 U.S. Highway 211 E
Luray, VA 22835-9036
(540) 999-3581
www.snpbooks.org

Dickey Ridge Visitor Center
Mile 4.6, Skyline Drive
Information, maps, permits, restrooms, water, books, films, exhibits

Harry F. Byrd, Sr. Visitor Center
Mile 51.0 at north entrance to Big Meadows
Information, maps, permits, restrooms, water, food, ranger programs, films, books, exhibits

Potomac Appalachian Trail Club (PATC, Inc.)
118 Park Street SE
Vienna, VA 22180
General information: (703) 242-0315
Fax: (703) 242-0968
www.patc.net
Office hours: Monday through Thursday, 7:00 to 9:00 P.M., and Thursday through Friday, noon to 2:00 P.M.

Appalachian Trail Conference (ATC)
Washington & Jackson Streets
P.O. Box 807
Harpers Ferry, WV 25425
(303) 535-6331

Ranger stations within the park:
North District: Mile 31.6 at Panorama
Central District: Mile 51.0 at Big Meadows (just before maintenance area)
South District: Mile 73.2 at Simmons Gap (east side of Skyline Drive)

The park has four entrance stations. Upon entering, you must purchase either an annual pass, a seven-day pass, or a National Parks pass. Fees vary from year to year.
Mile 0.6: Front Royal Entrance Station, just off U.S. Highway 340
Mile 31.5: Thornton Gap, U.S. Highway 211 interchange
Mile 65.5: Swift Run Gap, U.S. Highway 33 interchange
Mile 104.6: Rockfish Gap, Interstate 64 and U.S. Highway 250 interchange

Finding Maps

Several types of maps are available for the Shenandoah National Park hiker and can be obtained at the visitor centers, the waysides, and at sporting goods stores throughout the area, as well as purchased by writing or calling the map publishers: topographical maps, descriptive trail booklets, and free map handouts. All provide excellent information. However, the topographical maps are probably the most accurate. You would be wise to carry these, especially on extended trips, along with a good compass.

Providing completely accurate mileages of trails is difficult, however, so bear in mind that the trails may be slightly shorter or longer than indicated. In addition, the trail lengths on the maps sometimes differ from what is posted on the trail signs. Often more important than the actual length, though, is the difficulty rating. A very strenuous trail of 2 miles often does take longer than an easy one of 5 miles.

Free copies of some trail maps are available from the visitor center and the Shenandoah National Park Web site. The booklets for three short hikes can be obtained at the visitor centers, from the Shenandoah National Park Association, and in boxes at the trailheads. A minimal fee of $1.00 is charged for these booklets.

Quad and topographical maps may be purchased from the following sources:

Shenandoah National Park Association (see above)

Shenandoah National Park Visitor Centers (see above)

Trails Illustrated
Division of National Geographic Maps
P.O. Box 4357
Evergreen, CO 80437-4357
(800) 962-1643 or (303) 670-3457
Topographical Map 228 covers Shenandoah National Park.

Potomac Appalachian Trail Club (PATC, Inc.)
118 Park Street SE
Vienna, VA 22180
(703) 242-0315
Three PATC topographical maps (numbers 9, 10, and 11) cover Shenandoah National Park.

Waysides within Shenandoah National Park. Three waysides provide gas, oil, air, water, groceries, and camping and RV supplies and equipment. Hours of operation vary with the seasons. None of these waysides provide repairs. Elkwallow has a snack bar, Loft Mountain has breakfast and lunch, and Big Meadows has a restaurant.
Mile 24.0: Elkwallow Wayside
Mile 51.2: Big Meadows Wayside
Mile 79.5: Loft Mountain Wayside

U.S. Geological Survey (USGS)
National Mapping Division
12201 Sunrise Valley Drive, Mail Stop 809
Reston, VA 22092
(703) 648-7070
The USGS provides 1969 quad maps that do not contain current information such as trail modifications.

U.S. Geological Survey (USGS)
Branch of Distribution
Federal Center
Denver, CO 80225
Customer service: (800) 435-7627 or (303) 202-4200
The USGS provides 1969 quad maps that do not contain current information such as trail modifications.

Appendix B: Further Reading

The Shenandoah National Park Association makes available a wonderful selection of books for all ages. The visitor centers in the park also stock a great inventory of books for sale, as do the ARAMARK facilities along Skyline Drive. Topics available from these outlets include natural history, human history, mountain lore, hiking and backpacking, maps, children's books, and coloring books. The list of available resources is extensive.

Many of the following books were helpful as we prepared this book. Others make fascinating reading.

Amberson, Joanne. *Easy Hikes on the Appalachian National Scenic Trail in Shenandoah National Park*. Luray, Va.: Shenandoah National Park Association, 2003.

—. *Hikes to Peaks & Vistas in Shenandoah National Park*. Luray, Va.: Shenandoah National Park Association, 2002.

—. *Hikes to Waterfalls in Shenandoah National Park*. Luray, Va.: Shenandoah National Park Association, 1997.

—. *Short Hikes in Shenandoah National Park*. Luray, Va.: Shenandoah National Park Association, rev. 2004

Bell, C. Ritchie and Anne H. Lindsey. *Fall Color and Woodland Harvests*. Chapel Hill, N.C.: Laurel Hill Press, 1990.

Crandall, Hugh and Reed Engle. *Shenandoah: The Story Behind the Scenery*. Rev. ed. Las Vegas: KC Publications, Inc., 1997.

Engle, Reed. *Everything Was Wonderful: A Pictorial History of the Civilian Conservation Corps in Shenandoah National Park*. Luray, Va.: Shenandoah National Park Association, 1999.

—. *In the Light of the Mountain Moon: An Illustrated History of Skyland*. Luray, Va.: Shenandoah National Park Association, 2003.

Fletcher, Colin. *The Complete Walker*. New York: Alfred A. Knopf, 1971.

Harmon, Will. *Leave No Trace*. Helena, Mont.: Falcon, 1997.

—. *Wild Country Companion*. Helena, Mont.: Falcon, 1994.

Horning, Audrey. *In the Shadow of Ragged Mountain: Historical Archaeology of Nicholson, Corbin, & Weakley Hollows*. Luray, Va.: Shenandoah National Park Association, 2004.

Lambert, Darwin. *The Undying Past of Shenandoah National Park*. Boulder, Colo.: Roberts Rinehart Publishers, 1989.

Reeder, Carolyn and Jack Reeder. *Shenandoah Secrets: The Story of the Park's Hidden Past*. Vienna, Va.: Potomac Appalachian Trail Club, 1991.

Schneider, Bill. *Bear Aware*. Guilford, Conn.: The Globe Pequot Press, 2004.

Stupka, Arthur. *Wildflowers in Color*. New York: HarperCollins, 1994.

Watts, May Theilgaard. *Tree Finder: A Manual for the Identification of Trees by Their Leaves*. Rochester, N.Y.: Nature Study Guild, 1991.

Appendix C: Hike Index

Hike 58: Bear Den Mountain
Hike 59: Calf Mountain

Moderate Day Hikes

Hike 6: Compton Peak
Hike 15: Pine Hill Gap-Broad Hollow Loop
Hike 19: Hazel Falls and Cave
Hike 26: Hawksbill Summit
Hike 27: Rose River
Hike 31: Lewis Spring Falls Trail
Hike 38: South River Falls
Hike 39: Hightop Mountain Lariat
Hike 46: Frazier Discovery Trail
Hike 56: Turk Mountain
Hike 57: Jarman Gap to Beagle Gap

Strenuous Day Hikes

Hike 7: Mount Marshall Trail and Beyond
Hike 8: Keyser Run Fire Road-Little Devils Stairs Loop
Hike 11: Tuscarora-Overall Run Trail Loop
Hike 12: Thornton River
Hike 13: Knob Mountain-Jeremys Run Loop
Hike 16: Old Rag
Hike 18: Buck Hollow-Buck Ridge Trail Loop
Hike 20: Corbin Cabin Cutoff-Nicholson Hollow-Appalachian Trail Loop
Hike 25: Cedar Run-Whiteoak Canyon Loop
Hike 33: Rapidan Camp-Laurel Prong-Hazeltop Loop
Hike 42: Rocky Mount-Gap Run Lariat
Hike 43: Brown Mountain-Rocky Mountain Run Lariat
Hike 44: Ivy Creek
Hike 50: Austin Mountain-Furnace Mountain Loop
Hike 51: Rockytop
Hike 53: Trayfoot Mountain-Paine Run Loop
Hike 54: Moormans River
Hike 55: Riprap Trail

Backpacking Trips (one night or more)

Hike 7: Mount Marshall Trail and Beyond
Hike 11: Tuscarora-Overall Run Trail Loop
Hike 13: Knob Mountain-Jeremys Run Loop
Hike 16: Old Rag
Hike 50: Austin Mountain-Furnace Mountain Loop
Hike 51: Rockytop
Hike 55: Riprap Trail

Hikes with Great Views

Hike 7: Mount Marshall Trail and Beyond
Hike 9: Sugarloaf-Keyser Run Fire Road-Hogback Mountain Loop
Hike 16: Old Rag
Hike 17: Marys Rock
Hike 24: Bettys Rock and Crescent Rock
Hike 26: Hawksbill Summit
Hike 34: Bearfence Mountain
Hike 40: Powell Gap
Hike 52: Blackrock Summit
Hike 58: Bear Den Mountain

History Hikes

Hike 2: Fox Hollow Trail
Hike 3: Snead Farm-Dickey Ridge Trail Loop
Hike 10: Traces Trail
Hike 20: Corbin Cabin Cutoff-Nicholson Hollow-Appalachian Trail Loop
Hike 30: Big Meadows
Hike 36: Pocosin Trail

Hikes to See Waterfalls

Hike	Falls	Height in Feet	Skyline Mile
Hike 11	Overall Run Falls, upper falls	29	22.2
Hike 11	Overall Run Falls	93	22.2
Hike 25	Cedar Run Falls	34	45.6
Hike 25	Whiteoak Falls No. 1	86	45.6
Hike 25	Whiteoak Falls No. 2	62	45.6
Hike 25	Whiteoak Falls No. 3	35	45.6
Hike 25	Whiteoak Falls No. 4	41	45.6
Hike 25	Whiteoak Falls No. 5	49	45.6
Hike 25	Whiteoak Falls No. 6	60	45.6
Hike 27	Rose River Falls	67	49.4
Hike 28	Dark Hollow Falls	70	50.7
Hike 31	Lewis Spring Falls	81	51.2
Hike 38	South River Falls	83	62.8
Hike 49	Doyles River Falls No. 1	28	81.1
Hike 49	Doyles River Falls No. 2	63	81.1
Hike 49	Jones Run Falls	42	81.1

Appendix D: Where to Stay

Campgrounds

Four campgrounds are available in Shenandoah National Park, and they range from those with RV/camper spaces to tent sites, some of which are walk-in tent spaces. There is a fifth, primitive camping area, Dundo Group Camp, which is available to groups of eight to twenty persons by reservation only. Trailer hookups are not available in any of the campgrounds; however, all but Lewis Mountain have a disposal area. Obviously there is something for everyone. Big Meadows Campground requires reservations, so it's a good idea to call ahead, especially during the busier summer months. For those unable to plan ahead who find themselves in need of a campsite, it seems that unreserved sites become available early in the mornings as others pull out.

Backcountry or wilderness camping is allowed in most areas of the park. Those areas that are off-limits are listed for you in the handouts you acquire with the required backcountry camping permit, which can be obtained from the visitor centers or ranger stations.

From Skyline Drive, north to south, the campgrounds are as follows:

Mile 22.2: Mathews Arm Campground (179 sites). No reservations required. Flush toilets.

Mile 51.2: Big Meadows Campground (230 sites). Reservations system May through October. Can camp without reservations if the campground is not full. To reserve a site, talk with the folks at the campground entrance gate or call (800) 365–2267. Showers, camp store, laundry, water.

Mile 57.5: Lewis Mountain Campground (32 sites). First-come, first-served basis, tent and vehicle pull-in sites. Showers, camp store, water, laundry.

Mile 79.5: Loft Mountain Campground (219 sites). First-come, first-served basis, tent sites, RV sites, vehicle pull-ins. Showers, laundry, camp store, water.

Lodging Units

Lodging units for rent (best to make reservations) can be found at Mile 41.7, Skyland Resort, and Mile 51.2, Big Meadows. At Mile 57.5, Lewis Mountain, several cabins are available for rent. Remember that summer and fall are crowded, so call early (800-999-4714) to reserve. These are operated by ARAMARK, the official park concessioner. The lodging complexes have dining rooms and/or food service.

Shelters

Five shelters exist in the park. They are for day-use and emergency shelter only. Byrds Nest Shelter No. 4 is in the North District, while Byrds Nest Shelters No. 1, 2, and 3 and the Old Rag Shelter are in the Central District.

Huts

The Potomac Appalachian Trail Club (PATC) provides seven three-sided huts along the Appalachian Trail; these are intended mostly for Appalachian Trail long-distance hikers and are spaced about a day's hike (8 to 10 miles) apart. In emergencies other hikers may use the huts if they are not full. Otherwise, you must camp out of sight of the hut unless different regulations are posted at the hut sites.

Cabins

The PATC also owns and maintains six cabins scattered throughout the park. Information on renting them and what is supplied may be obtained by contacting the PATC office at 118 Park Street SE, Vienna, VA 22180; general information: (703) 242-0315, fax: (703) 242-0968.

About the Authors

Bert Gildart has been writing about the outdoors for more than twenty years. For thirteen summers he served as a backcountry ranger in Glacier National Park. He has written more than 300 magazine articles for such publications as *Smithsonian, Travel & Leisure, Modern Maturity, Field & Stream,* and *National Wildlife.* Together, Bert and his wife, Jane, have hiked hundreds of miles throughout many wilderness and backcountry areas of the country. They have collaborated on several other FalconGuides including: *Best Easy Day Hikes Shenandoah National Park, A FalconGuide to Death Valley National Park, A FalconGuide to Dinosaur National Monument, Best Easy Day Hikes Black Hills Country,* and *Hiking the Black Hills Country.*